AN INTRODUCTION TO

Tantra and Sacred Sexuality

MICHAEL MIRDAD

AN INTRODUCTION TO

Tantra and Sacred Sexuality

MICHAEL MIRDAD

GRAIL
PRESS

AN INTRODUCTION TO
Tantra and Sacred Sexuality

GRAIL
PRESS

PO Box 1908
Sedona, AZ 86339
(360) 671-8349

office@grailproductions.com
www.SpiritualTantra.net
www.GrailProductions.com

Cover and Interior Design by Robert Lanphear
Illustration by Richard Bulman

Library of Congress Cataloging-in-Publication Data
Mirdad, Michael.
An Introduction to Tantra and Sacred Sexuality/ Michael Mirdad.
Library of Congress Control Number: 2008907846
ISBN 978-0-9740216-3-8
1. Sexuality 2. Tantra 3. Relationships 4. Self-help 5. New Age
I. Title: An Introduction to Tantra and Sacred Sexuality. II. Title

THIRD EDITION

DISCLAIMER: The concepts shared in this book are merely ideas and beliefs held within the
various arts of sacred sexuality. Because we are all so different, some of the concepts, exercises
or techniques may be agreeable to you and others may not. Whatever the case, choose what
works for you and integrate it into your own personal life and sexual practice. If you have any
questions or concerns regarding your mental or physical health, please consult a professional.
The author and publisher are not responsible for any affects this material may have.

Table of Contents

Chapter 4 • Modern Practices of Sacred Sex

PART III • SELF-AWARENESS

Chapter 5 • Know Thyself

PART IV • INTIMACY WITH OTHERS

Chapter 6 • Foreplay

Chapter 7 • Intercourse

PART VII • SUMMARY AND CONCLUSION

Chapter 10 • Now for the Best Part

PART VIII • APPENDIX

TO THE READER

Most of the material in this book is
also found in Michael Mirdad's book
entitled *Sacred Sexuality: A Manual
for Living Bliss*, which is an extended
version that contains numerous
diagrams, exercises, and techniques.

Acknowledgments

My prayers of thanksgiving go out to all of my friends and supporters. Thanks to Lynne Matous for her editing, as well as to Robin, Gregg, Jackie, Ron and everyone else who took the time to assist with editing and proofreading the manuscript. My deepest thanks also goes to the many teachers and authors who have practiced and taught an authentic form of sacred sexuality including Valerie Brooks, Mantak Chia, David A. Ramsdale, Diana Richardson, and Osho. Lastly, I extend my deepest appreciation to all of the students who have attended my sacred sexuality workshops and to everyone who added to this book by adding to my life and to my understanding of the sacredness of sexuality (and of life itself).

I dedicate this book to our Divine Creator and to the Love that permeates all things.

Cover and Interior Design by
Robert Lanphear

Illustrations by
Richard Bulman
www.BulmanFineArt.com

Foreword

Beyond his accomplishments as international spiritual leader, healer, and author, Michael Mirdad is a man with a heart of gold. During our first encounter, the quality that I felt emanating from him was a sense of balance. Michael is confident with a soft humility, serious with a child's playfulness, and complex with a zen-like simplicity. He has the rare ability to take himself and, consequently, his students beyond the titles, categories, and limitations that society or we ourselves tend to erect and into the grace of truth. He is courageously and thoroughly expansive, challenging himself and others to live in the full aliveness of the present moment.

In *An Introduction to Tantra and Sacred Sexuality*, Michael gently applies such courage to our most vulnerable and intimate of resources: our sexuality. Based on over twenty years as a healer and leader, his approach is simple, yet not easy. It is about walking the balance of saturated ecstasy, while at the same time being nonattached. It is about loving all parts of ourselves and yet knowing that we are so much more than the sum of those parts. Michael's teachings embrace the joy inherent in all aspects of ourselves, our lives, and our worlds. Then they take us even deeper.

An Introduction to Tantra and Sacred Sexuality eases us through the historical myriads of sexual behaviors, philosophies, and methodologies that span many thousands of years, combining wisdom from both the traditional and the esoteric. By distilling the essence of each, Michael leads us to an essential truth within ourselves. This truth, which is our birthright, affirms our sexual innocence, forever-expanding aliveness, and giddy bliss. Michael shows us how to *live* the sacredness of sexuality within our relationships, during our moments alone, and throughout our everyday lives. His book applies equally to those with healthy sexual patterns who seek more profound levels of ecstasy and to those still healing from sexual trauma. From the multi-orgasmic to the non-orgasmic, Michael considers each man and woman. He honors where we are now and provides the safety for who we know we can become.

Prepare for the profound and ecstatic treats that await your senses in the following pages. *An Introduction to Tantra and Sacred Sexuality* is not simply a manual for sexuality; it is a guide for living in sexual balance and spiritual grace.

Valerie Brooks,
  Author, *Tantric Awakening*

Preface

It would be difficult to understand and appreciate who you are, your destiny, or your True Nature if you omitted any part of yourself, even the most human part—your sexual self. This book takes you on a journey through a vital part of your sacred self—your sexuality. It offers insights on how to awaken and integrate your whole being, resulting in a union of your body and soul with the Spirit of the Divine.

An Introduction to Tantra and Sacred Sexuality offers insights into how to live ecstatically by awakening your sensual self and sharing this presence with others, moment-by-moment. This book does not promote *one* particular style of sexuality over another. Instead, it is a synthesis of many of the ancient arts combined with modern principles of sex and sexual healing. Therefore, you will discover that this book is exciting and enticing, as well as powerful and healing.

You do not have to be in a relationship to enjoy, apply, and explore sacred sexuality or this book. In this book, the term *partner* does not exclusively refer to someone with whom you have a committed relationship. Rather, it refers to the person with whom you are sharing the particular experience.

The terminology in this material is kept simple to avoid overwhelming the reader with ancient terminology and excessive use of Sanskrit words. One exception to this rule is that throughout most of the book, Sanskrit words are used for the penis (*lingam,* meaning "Wand of Light") and vagina (*yoni,* meaning "Sacred Space").

Finally, some spiritual teachings insist that you must set aside your body to find your soul. This book, on the other hand, shares the philosophy of *A Course in Miracles,* which suggests that before you can experience *universal* love, you must first remove the obstacles and judgments keeping it veiled. In other words, before you can feel your *universal* body, you must first love every particle of your *physical* body. Then, after lovingly reclaiming your total body and receiving the gift of love from the universe, you will discover that a whole new life awaits you.

To the pure in heart, everything is pure.

—Kaulavali Nirnaya Tantra

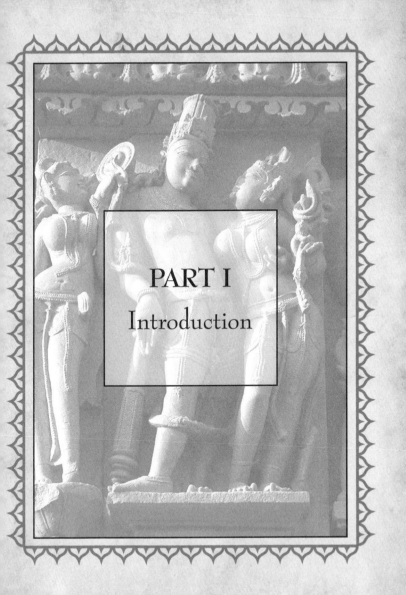

PART I
Introduction

The Sacred Sexual Experience

Taking Sex to a Whole New Level

*I*magine how it feels physically, emotionally, **energetically and spiritually to have the love essence of every molecule, atom, and sub-atomic particle in the universe dancing with delight as they rejoin similar love essences within your being.** The energetic response is ecstatic! Practicing sacred sexuality and channeling loving energy are highly effective ways to raise our vibrations to the level of embodied "gods and goddesses."

Science teaches that our physical bodies are not as dense as they appear and that there is more *space* within our bodies than there is *density*. Sacred sexuality is about sharing and exploring an intimate relationship with this inner spaciousness beyond the dense, material body. It's a state of living in the vibration of the soul. It's about accessing our souls—the parts of us that remember bliss beyond measure. Afterwards, everything we do becomes an experience of union with All That Is.

Orgasm is a state where your body is no longer felt as matter; it vibrates like energy, electricity. It vibrates so deeply, from the very foundation, that you completely forget that it is a material thing. In orgasm, you come to this deepest layer of your body where matter no longer exists, just energy waves; you become a dancing energy, vibrating.

—Osho

Technically, all sex is sacred, as are all souls, but not everyone treats it that way. Nevertheless, irresponsible use of sexuality does not remove the sacredness but merely veils our ability to see and experience it. The term "sacred sexuality" has many closely related meanings. But since the word *sacred* refers to "the spirit" and *sexuality* refers to "the body," the two words combined describe a merging of the worlds of spirit and matter, or the soul with the body.

Sacred sexuality is about experiencing levels of ecstatic bliss and unconditional love (usually only attainable through prolonged practice of advanced meditation techniques) and, most importantly, bringing these experiences into our daily lives. It's ultimately about *living* bliss, not just *feeling* it. In practicing sacred sexuality, we learn to live *within* the material world while integrating an experience and vibration *beyond* this world—one that feels ecstatic and almost uncontainable. This vibration translates into consistently feeling unconditional love for all people and things, which is why it is called "the path of living bliss."

In sacred sexuality, all aspects (physical, energetic, emotional, mental, and spiritual) of our beings are utilized to arouse the fullest sexual experience possible. In other words, these various aspects of consciousness are brought to full awakening and enhanced by the sexual experience: the physical body with its senses and sensations, the energetic body with its energy systems and kundalini, the emotional body with its romance and desires, the mental body with its fantasies and focus, and the spiritual body with its love and divine awareness. All are utilized to increase arousal. Afterwards, each aspect of consciousness, in turn, is brought to another level of awareness.

During a truly sacred sexual experience, our attention moves beyond the sexual anatomy and into the eyes and hearts of our partners. With this higher focus, we become keenly aware that our partners are more than bodies. **As our relationships deepen, it becomes easier to open our hearts and allow our partners into the sacred spaces of our souls.** With the increased depth and sacredness of the sexual experience, passion and spontaneity are not lost. On the contrary, they are enhanced. This deepening trust creates an openness to, and desire for, the experiences of passion and spontaneity. Then, sexual ecstasy occurs at the point when our bodies are merging with spirit, as we disappear as individuals and become one with everything. Contrary to most beliefs, the true practitioners of sacred sexuality are not obsessing on nor expecting sexual intercourse. Instead, they are using the act of sensual expression as a means to unveil themselves—on their own or with (one or more) others—and are doing so with the most vulnerable aspect of their beings, their sexual selves.

In general, there are four potential stages to a sacred sexual experience. Anyone who chooses to explore a sacred sexual experience might do so by selecting any *one* of these stages or by applying *all* of them. Whichever the case, there are a few general stages to any sexual encounter. Although the first few stages are crucial, it is common to neglect the fourth step, postplay (the afterglow), which is as important as any of the others. Although any single part is enough by itself, the most complete experience goes through the following four stages:

1. Foreplay: building connection and enjoying arousal
2. Intercourse: practicing some form of sexual pleasuring
3. Orgasm: experiencing some level of release
4. Postplay: enjoying the afterglow

Reclaiming Love, Desire, and Passion

Ultimately, love is both the goal *of* and results *from* healthy, intimate sharing. Indeed, one of the most profound expressions of love is intimacy (meaning "in-to-me-see"). Intimacy, therefore, results from the mutual desire to love, the yearning to share, and the willingness to be vulnerable. **Where two or more are gathered with one common goal of love, *there* is the Presence of God.** Sacred sexuality is an ideal meeting place for discovering the greater depths of intimacy. Therefore, how, when, where, and with whom we share sexual expression is worth much consideration.

Since true sexual union is based on harmony, it is important to understand that complete cooperation, communication, and agreement are a must. If the two are truly one, then there will be a great deal of sensitivity for the likes and dislikes of each partner. So, in effect, sexual union can enhance sensitivity and compassion for self and others.

There are three active forces within the human consciousness that assist us in expressing and experiencing profound and intimate relationships with others. These forces are LOVE (with our hearts), DESIRE (with our feelings), and PASSION or sexuality (with our bodies). During intimate relationships with others, most people experience only one or two of these forces at any given time. Yet, the ideal scenario for the deepest experience of soul-sharing between partners is to have all three of these forces in harmonious balance.

Love is what we really are at the level of the soul. To share the heart and soul, we must be evolved enough to hold the presence of love within *our own* hearts, first and foremost. To share heart and soul with another, we must be courageous enough to accept vulnerability at its deepest level, or to love even at the risk of being hurt.

Desire can serve as a bridge between love and sex, or the heart and the body. The desire we feel is an accurate gauge of the vitality and spontaneity present in our lives and relationships. Desire acts as wood for the fire of passion. Desire without love can result in longing and neediness.

Passion and Sexuality are most fully expressed when accompanied by love and healthy desire. *Love* in its healthiest physical manifestation can be referred to as *sacred sexuality*. **In the art of sacred sexuality, the bodies meet to physically express what is felt in the hearts and souls.** This does not mean that all sexual experiences must necessarily be between two individuals who are "in love." Rather, the ideal goal is for both partners to maintain a space of loving presence within *themselves* and responsibly choose with whom to share this love. If both partners *are* emotionally healthy and responsible, this loving presence, in turn, can help to create a sacred union for both to experience.

When we join with others in sexual expression while maintaining a healthy balance of love, desire, and sexual passion, we will experience and share one of life's greatest gifts—an alchemical fusion of spirit and body. But this experience is also contingent upon possessing emotional and spiritual maturity. If maturity is present, we will choose the right partners, those who match our own levels of consciousness.

The Essentials of Sacred Sexuality

A spiritual approach to sexuality can be immensely freeing for anyone who usually focuses on quick orgasms and shallow expressions of sex. Sacred sexuality offers an expansive experience based on mutual love, acceptance, and authenticity.

Sacred sexuality allows us to deepen pleasure, have orgasms in more ways than one, and broaden our ideas of pleasuring beyond, but not excluding, intercourse. It also deepens the purpose of lovemaking beyond bodily connecting to include joining emotionally and spiritually with our partners. With a willingness to bring our higher selves (hearts and souls) to the sharing of our emotions and bodies, we reach new levels of Divine Presence.

Unless you go beyond your biology, you will never know your soul.

—Osho

The practice of sacred sexuality requires enough self-awareness and maturity to follow a few simple principles (with love and respect as the foundation throughout) *and* to set healthy boundaries. The essential principles are as follows:

1. *Safety*–You must feel safe and supported at all times. Both partners must be committed to protecting each other's well-being. Safety includes never asking for, or engaging in, any sexual behavior that feels physically or psychologically painful, scary, or unsafe. Furthermore, a loving partner would not ask otherwise and will understand if and when you say "NO." Safety also paves the way for open and honest communication.

2. *Responsibility*–You, the practitioner, are in charge of your own beliefs and decisions. In the practice of sacred sexuality, you are the one who decides with whom you share and in what form. So choose well!

3. *Communication*–Once you are healthy enough to create *safety* and mature enough to take *responsibility*, it's time to deepen *communication*. Your needs must be expressed (using words, sounds, and gestures). In sacred

sex, communication is done in a loving manner, by showing reverence for the other person and by accentuating the positives. Healthy communication is never judgmental, critical, or condescending, but *is* loving, sincere, and constructive. Practicing healthy communication encourages you to push through apprehension and express erotic sensations in any form that feels authentic, such as sensual moans and groans.

4. *Trust and Surrender*–Without establishing these few essential principles, or guidelines, you will not feel comfortable enough to completely trust, let go, and surrender. But, within the boundaries of the above guidelines, you will be free to surrender to greater heights and depths of loving, living, and being. Developing greater trust in yourself and your healthy decision-making (as well as your partner's) is a major step on the path to *living bliss*.

The Goals of Sacred Sexuality

If sex, in and of itself, were magically transforming, there would be a lot of enlightened porn-stars in the world. On the contrary, without a spiritual and loving intent, sex limits the expression of our True Self and becomes a form of self-condemnation. In other words, sex without depth of consciousness is not only valueless but destructive as well. Conscious sex, on the other hand, is one of the finest rewards on the path to enlightenment. When practicing sacred, conscious sex, you are encouraged to access the core of love within your being, discover deeper aspects of yourself, and then share with another if you so choose. When sharing sacred sexuality with a partner, you develop a deeper love and respect for each other, while creating and experiencing greater quantities of ecstatic energy throughout the nervous system.

The exploration of sacred sexuality is not a means for self-gratification or the fulfillment of ego-centered goals or pleasures. Instead, it's a method for playfully discovering ways to learn about yourself and others while connecting with Spirit. Paradoxically, this spiritual connection is accomplished by living the Divine *through* your physical life, rather than by *escaping* that same physical life.

The sensual pleasure women provide, the joy of wine, the taste of meat: it is the undoing of fools, but for the wise, the pathway to salvation.

—*Kalarnava Tantra*

When truly walking the "spiritual path," you perceive all things as sacred including sexuality. Perceiving all things as sacred, you no longer evaluate the world and other beings with your senses and then formulate opinions. Instead, you understand and know that all experiences perceived by the physical senses originate in the soul of the perceiver, which frees you to *experience through* your senses, rather than *judge with* them. So every dance you dance (or experience you have) is not really with another person; it simply reflects a meeting with yourself.

If we perceive ourselves as separate from the wholeness of Spirit, we will undoubtedly search for our completion *in* others. This longing to find wholeness through others is an unhealthy manifestation of desire. Once we find the object of our search, for example, we desire to possess it (or them). Now we are approaching the world as predators, seeking to capture anyone or anything that might "complete" us. When one hostage proves unfulfilling, we seek out and capture another person or object. This endless cycle of codependent behavior is the most rampant form of addiction on earth.

Objectifying, or treating other human beings as objects, diminishes them and us. Even Jesus, the Christ, took a moment to explain the limitations of looking upon a woman with objectifying lust. He expressed that **any man who looks at a woman only as a means of fulfillment, does not see the woman herself, but merely an object of potential pleasure. In doing so, he misses the essence of who she is, the treasures she holds in her heart, and the**

potential their relationship offers. The same principle applies for how a woman views and treats a man.

Eventually, failing to find fulfillment in others, we begin to realize that what we desire is not an object or person outside of ourselves. What we really desire and long for is a union with God. This realization redefines our old, limiting, negative concepts about desire. It awakens a truer, clearer understanding of the desire to re-member the dis-membered parts of our being.

Finally, we discover that it is futile to excessively displace our desires onto any one person or thing, since desire (as an attribute of love, or God) is a force that exists among all things. Therefore, to single out any one person or thing as the object of our love (when that same love could be felt for all people and things) often makes that very person an obstacle to our experiencing a God-like fluidity of loving consciousness. Nevertheless, we can still choose to demonstrate a unique—even monogamous— love for one person, as this experience can also be a vehicle for developing unconditional love. But even the most amazing monogamous relationship has its potential traps. For example, when a single person (or object) takes an exclusive place in our hearts, we tend to reach for that person with longing, which indicates that we perceive something missing within our own being. In such cases, love is no longer expansive and unconditional, but becomes contracted and fear-based, which always results in pain and suffering.

On the other hand, when our love is directed to *all* beings, *all* life, and *all* space, the flow of our awareness remains expansive. We no longer have a desire to own or control. Instead, we are free to love and be loved—to share love because we *are* love. In this expansive state of being, lack and aloneness are nonexistent. Here, we can make a centered decision to share with one or more people. The ideal is to feel love for all and then choose how, and with whom, to demonstrate this love. To live and love in this state of consciousness is to live and love as God. **Desire is now experienced as a unifying force and vibration felt in and through all things—ultimately experienced as an emotion of God.**

Now you are free to observe and relate to a person (or an object) with unconditional, unattached love and acceptance, with no desire for ownership or possession. In such a relationship, there are no agendas, but there *can* be deep sharing. The choice to see clearly, through the eyes of unconditional love, is the choice to see Divinely. Such vision enables the gift of a person's true identity to emerge. Again, accessing this gift involves being with, but not possessing, another person; love is shared between hearts and souls rather than egos.

This new level of unconditional love and awareness helps you realize that you do not, and cannot, love or hate another because there is no *other* separate from you. Instead, your interactions with others either reflect self-love or self-betrayal. As your understanding of love (of your true goodness) develops, you find that **since everyone you meet is a part of you, you are now safe to love everyone and everything.** As you begin to realize that you *are* love, you no longer participate in needy-love with another. Rather, the love you *are* desires to express and experience itself; and in so doing, this love is expanded. **As you awaken to your natural vibration of love, every particle of universal love is drawn to you.** So activities like drinking water or breathing air are no longer perceived as the meeting of your needs. Instead, they are the irresistible joining of two parts of the same whole.

It is all right to enjoy life; the secret of happiness is not to become attached to anything. Enjoy the smell of the flower, but see God in it.

—Paramahansa Yogananda

Once you gain a fuller understanding of true, unconditional love, your entire being undergoes a process of awakening. This awakening includes the physical body (sexual anatomy and physiology), energy systems, and emotional body. The awakening of these multiple levels of consciousness is not always chronological or necessarily permanent. Instead, it's much like any other form of evolution: You continually learn, expand, grow, and awaken to newer and deeper levels of awareness.

The practice of sacred sexuality can be summarized as a process designed to deepen your connection to the Spirit of Love and to awaken your physical body—allowing this temple to become as passionate and alive as God originally intended it to be.

The glory of God is human beings fully alive.

—Irenaeus (Bishop of Lyons)

The numerous advantages to developing a healthy sexual life offer incalculable gifts. These advantages include the following:

1. Getting in touch with your own body and soul, which results in . . .
2. Leading a healthier life with greater self-awareness, which results in . . .
3. Developing your own healthy boundaries and sexuality, which results in . . .
4. Awakening deeper connections with the hearts and souls of others, which results in . . .

5. Developing a greater ability to explore and enjoy the bodies of others, which results in . . .
6. Reaching deeper levels of love, intimacy, and passion, which results in . . .
7. Attaining sustained levels of ecstasy and bliss, which results in . . .
8. Encouraging unconditional love and limitless expansion of consciousness, which results in . . .
9. Integrating the energy and lessons experienced during all sacred sexual encounters, which results in . . .
10. Returning to number one and raising each of the aforementioned to a higher level . . .

The Reasons Men and Women Learn Tantra or Sacred Sexuality

The reasons for exploring any aspect of sacred sexuality (including Tantra) may be one or many—some reasons being more profound than others. Furthermore, there are truly some wonderful tantric practitioners with the highest regard for this sacred practice. Such practitioners (*tantrikas*) are capable of facilitating incredible experiences for their students and clients. Nevertheless, the student or client should walk this path carefully, as there are far too many so-called "teachers and healers" who use the name of Tantra or sacred sexuality to disguise actions resulting from their own unhealed wounds and sexual addictions. Therefore, choosing a teacher or healer should be a responsible and well-thought-out process.

The following reasons (listed from the most common, yet least profound, to the least common, yet most profound) are why both men and women choose to learn Tantra or sacred sexuality:

1. To satisfy sexual addictions (usually unknowingly).
2. To improve sexual performance.
3. To increase the connection between partners.
4. To explore the compulsions stemming from possible past life memories of a sensual lifestyle.
5. To use sacred sexuality as a means of sexual healing.
6. To use sacred sexuality as a means of deepening spiritual life.
7. To explore Tantra or sacred sexuality (in its most authentic sense) as a spiritual path.

The Heights of Sex Versus the Depths of Sex

It's not uncommon for people to describe their more favorable sexual experiences as "great sex." Yet, few have any idea how *great* a sexual experience can be. Those who do, however, would probably find it indescribable because truly great sex involves love, passion, trust, intimacy, and even cosmic experiences. Ironically, according to statistics, what is commonly called "great sex" usually does not occur with established partners or mates, but with someone with whom there is little or no emotional investment. From the standpoint of sacred sexuality, however, an encounter without *caring* and *feeling* would never be described as a "great" experience.

Even many professional sexologists maintain that the best sex is usually experienced with a temporary lover and not a mate. Unfortunately, for many individuals, this is true. But these misguided individuals have to separate heart from pelvis, spirit from body, and love from sex. Once they get used to this unhealthy behavior, they rarely think to look back to discover what they've missed.

One deceptive aspect of sexual heights is that this type of sexual energy can appear to manifest in people who seem sexually healthy, but their sexual motivation arises from, and is affected by, unhealthy parts of their being. One well-known example is Marilyn Monroe, who projected the image of the definitive sexual goddess but claimed to have never had an orgasm—undoubtedly due to her history of unhealed sexual abuse.

Another example of trouble brewing under the surface of a seemingly healthy sexual nature is that of a woman who is attracted to the "dangerous type" of man. This attraction is not based on "real" love. On the contrary, in an attempt to dance with her demons, the woman feels irresistibly drawn beyond the zone of safety. This very attempt to access and release her repressed emotions is capable of creating sexual stimulation and orgasms. A man and woman assume there is something "special" about an *edgy* relationship because they get so aroused. But some of this *specialness* and orgasmic energy comes from the unseen levels of emotion that are triggered and need to be released.

Generally speaking, **there are two different types of sexual experiences. One focuses on what might be called the "heights of sex," often referred to as "great sex," while the other accesses the "depths" of sex, which is sacred sexuality.** A relationship that emphasizes the *heights* of sex focuses mainly on stimulation and nervous system response. This experience is known as merely "having sex." It is referred to in yogic traditions as *tamas*, or sex of a shallow consciousness. It arises from unfulfilled fantasy and addictive behaviors, rather than from conscious sharing with a partner. It stresses quantity over quality. The heights of the sexual experience are usually measured by the intensity and quantity of stimulation and the success of orgasms, which is like judging the *quality* of food by the *quantity* ingested. Such stimulation has a "hot" energy and is focused on excitation of the clitoris or penis, while the *depths* of sex have a "warm or cool" energy and focus on the ecstasy released between the heart, as well as the energetic aspects of the genitals.

Encounters focusing on the heights of sex could be defined as physically intense and stimulating, but emotionally and spiritually shallow. The heights of sex imply "more is better," which translates as faster and bigger—larger breasts, a bigger penis, harder thrusting, and louder cries of pleasure. These experiences can also be present in the depths of sex, but as a secondary priority and without the need, goal, and obsession for such.

Physical . . . sex doesn't even come close to the incredible bliss of Heaven . . . It's very similar to a narcotic. Heaven, on the other hand, is a perfect, indescribable ecstasy that never ceases . . . Imagine the very peak of a perfect sexual orgasm, except this orgasm never stops. It keeps going on forever with no decrease in its powerful and flawless intensity.

—Gary Renard

(*The Disappearance of the Universe*)

A relationship focusing on the *depths* of sex, on the other hand, accesses the soul of both partners. It is known as "making love," and is referred to in yogic traditions as *sattva*, or sex that is holistic. The depths of sex encourage both partners to make use of their bodies, minds, and souls to access each other's heart. This type of interaction between partners provides the safety to explore the darker issues and inhibitions that may arise during a truly intimate sexual experience. In essence, the depths of sex involve a union of body, mind, and soul. Within this deeper, more authentic sexual experience, heights *can* be attained. Again, all of the great sensations and spontaneity of the heights of sex are possible but from a level of maturity, responsibility, and conscious awareness.

The heights of sex stir us to quickly remove the clothes of our lovers before having sex. The depths of sex encourage us to dress them afterwards. The heights draw us to kiss them numerous times on the way to orgasm, but the depths stir us to kiss them afterwards. The heights stir us to reach for their genitals, but the depths encourage us to reach for their hearts.

Warning: Sex Feels Good

Before proceeding further, it should be noted that both the heights *and* depths of sex can be very addictive. Yet you need not become addicted. On the contrary, the primary purpose of this book is to teach you how to practice spiritual, responsible sex with the goal of using sex to learn about—not escape from—yourself. Sexual addiction and other forms of shallow sex often result from a desire to hide or escape from issues that need healing.

The reason that sexual *depths* can be addictive is easily understandable. Although sexual heights offer intense levels of sexual stimulation that can leave us wanting more, the depths of sex offer a connection of body, mind, and soul that can be all encompassing. In other words, although stimulation can feel good, bliss feels great! Experiencing the depths of sexual bliss, especially for the first time, feels like the voice of God calling us home. There is an undeniable sense of completeness. We long to make this experience an integrated part of our lives. Of course, we can also become attached to anyone (partners, healers or teachers) who assists us in this awakening, but as we make this blissful state a part of our own consciousness, we realize that attaching our feelings to others is pointless.

On the other hand, the potential addictions behind sexual *heights* are rooted in personal dysfunction. **Behind every shallow sexual interaction, there hides a person who does**

not want to see or be seen at a deeper level. In such cases, sex is used as a distraction. Despite the obvious physical connection of a sexual encounter, the act itself in this case is used to remain distant from, not join with, another. It makes little difference how intense the attraction might be. In fact, often the stronger the attraction, the stronger the dysfunction. This seeming enigma can be explained by the fact that our egos attract others who appear to have the power to fulfill us or whom we can blame for our lack of happiness and fulfillment. With such a deceptively promising prospect behind relationships, it's no wonder our attractions often manifest as a yearning or ache in the mind, body, and soul.

Hidden behind the potential addiction to sexual depths is a longing to experience heaven. Hidden behind the potential addiction to sexual heights is a decision to remain in hell.

Again, we become distracted by sexual attraction for others as a way to avoid some painful ache within our own beings. Shallow-level sex can be an easy, enticing distraction. The stimulation feels good, but there's a "cat and mouse" ego game involved, whereby we hunt and trap those whom we think will fill our hunger. It's a game for the dysfunctional that takes place in the fantasy of the mind. Although we are guaranteed to go home with someone, we always wake up more alone than the night before. With an intensified level of pain, we try again with someone else, and soon the obsession grows. **Until we realize that _we_ are the "other person" we've been looking for, others will eventually leave us feeling empty.**

The shallow or addictive encounter can never produce what it promises. The quality of a building always depends on its blueprint. If you enter an encounter believing you are lacking something, you will experience this very lack. If you _bargain_ away your body to get love, self-worth, or anything else, inevitably you will come out empty-handed. It is impossible to discover your True Self (which is Love) by sharing an encounter that lacks love, safety, vulnerability, and emotional honesty. It cannot be done!

Behind every dysfunctional choice, there is a misdirected call for love. It is your cry to the world that you want to find yourself. But you don't know where to look, or you believe that you will not like what you find if you look inside. Nevertheless, be of good cheer. The answer (Love) is as close as your own heart.

The Complete Orgasmic Experience

Every human being is completely unique—physically, energetically, emotionally, mentally, and spiritually. Therefore, the types of orgasms that each human being experiences are unique. In other words, **no two human**

beings experience exactly the same kinds of orgasm. Furthermore, no single human being has exactly the same orgasm on more than one occasion.

There are generally two types of orgasm: physical "peak" and soul-level "valley." The peak involves *stimulation and excitation* and is goal-oriented. The valley involves *pleasuring and relaxation* and is non-goal-oriented. The peak orgasm involves much effort from the one pleasuring and more tensing and anticipation by the receiver as he or she builds toward orgasm and/or ejaculation. The valley orgasm, on the other hand, involves slower movements and fuller consciousness. There are no distracting goals because the present moment is all that matters. The peak orgasm is quick to reach and quicker to pass. The valley orgasm can take minutes or hours and can last for hours or even days. With a peak, you *have* an orgasm. But with a valley, you *are* orgasmic.

A physical, or peak, orgasm is related more to the penis and clitoris, while a full-body, or valley, orgasm addresses the whole body, including the nerves, organs, blood, glands, and marrow of bones. In a peak orgasm, the energy moves down and out of the body in compliance with our nature to procreate. Most of the sensation and stimulation is around the genitals. On the other hand, with a valley orgasm, the energy moves upward and inward, spreading throughout the body in compliance with our nature to *be* creators and to connect with the Creator within. Furthermore, although valley orgasms have fewer contractions and physical sensations, they take you deeper into your soul. They create a feeling of floating or being filled with liquid or energetic waves. Although external, or peak, orgasms rarely result in internal, or valley, orgasms, it is possible to have both, providing the internal orgasm is given priority.

There are three other types of orgasm that bridge the seemingly irreconcilable differences between peak and valley orgasms. These bridges are the *energetic* orgasm, the *emotional* orgasm, and the *mental* orgasm. The first stage beyond the physical orgasm is the energetic orgasm—commonly chosen by Taoist practitioners of sacred sexuality. Choosing the level of orgasm you would like to experience involves consciously channeling the sexual energy of the groin upward through the body.

Peak or valley orgasms (as well as any other level of orgasm) can be experienced individually or in combination with any other type. Again, you can either consciously choose the level (or type) of orgasms you would like to experience, or you can just allow them to unfold as they may. Whichever the case, **all orgasms are wonderful, in part, because they create a sense of openness, vulnerability, release, and connection**. Orgasms can also be used to redirect sexual energy into higher levels of consciousness.

There is one remaining level of orgasm beyond the description of the first five. This is the SPIRITUAL ORGASM, achieved only through self-discipline and the highest spiritual initiations.

Aside from the various *levels* of orgasm (which correspond to states of human consciousness), there are different *types* of orgasm as well. These include the following:

1. The "not sure if I had one" is a non-distinct sensation that occurs more often for women. This orgasm can include variations of energetic or emotional releases.
2. Peak orgasm (with or without ejaculation).
3. In-jaculations are an evolved form of peak orgasms.
4. Multiple orgasms can be several individual orgasms or many groups of orgasms.
5. Valley orgasms shift from something you *do* (or have done) to something you *experience* as you surrender into blissful waves of ecstasy. They usually manifest as total-being orgasms.

When Your Body Doesn't Cooperate

Since most books on sexuality appear to assume that all men and women are orgasmic or even multi-orgasmic, it's important to discuss those individuals whose bodies seem to be shut down and are having difficulty having orgasms. This lack of response might last for a day, or it may be an ongoing issue. If you experience this lack of response, rest assured that you are not alone and that there is hope.

The constant flood of articles and media coverage saying that you are incomplete, not functioning normally, or missing out when you do not experience "sufficient" orgasms is a double-edged sword. On one hand, it can open your mind to new ideas of what you could add to your life. On the other hand, it can make you feel incomplete as a man or woman and disheartened over the condition of your sexual life. Such feelings are especially prevalent in women.

So let's begin by saying that **every man and woman has had some form of orgasm.** It may have been during sleep. It may have been an unnoticed quiver or perhaps a tear of release forming in the eye. Nevertheless, these responses must be accepted as valid forms of energetic release before greater sensations can be experienced.

Comparing your sexual experiences with those of other people is a waste of energy. In fact, a woman is likely to be increasingly frustrated when hearing about women who have multiple orgasms when she can't even manage to have *one* on a consistent basis. It's equally frustrating for a man to hear about other men who manage to make love for prolonged periods without prematurely ejaculating when he cannot make it through the first few minutes. By featuring only success stories, the books, magazines, and videos on sexuality are very misleading and often leave the reader feeling "left out." But these men and women are not alone. In fact, they are part of a huge majority. After all, only thirty percent of women recently surveyed claimed to have orgasms during intercourse, and only half that number claimed to have ever experienced multiple orgasms. As for men, the average male is said to ejaculate within the first five minutes of intercourse.

There are reasons why some men and women's bodies do not open up to orgasm as easily as others do. These causes include the following:

1. Lack of anatomical knowledge
2. Lack of intuitive sensitivity
3. Lack of patience and relaxation
4. Lack of comfort with a particular partner
5. Unhealed wounds residing in the mind or body

After experiencing repeated frustration from a lack of response to sexual stimulation, a person's body tends to shut down even more. Then the mind and emotions suffer from disappointment, causing a person to lose interest in sex altogether. An often overlooked reason for sexual shutdown in a woman is that women have learned to experience sex like men—thinking that *harder and quicker* is the way to sexual fulfillment. This behavior is contrary to their "yin" nature, which calls for a deepening, relaxed, fuller experience. In other words, experiencing the heights of sex, with all its flare, passion, and intensity, often has a detrimental effect on a woman's body. It tends to desensitize her, leaving her needing more stimulation the next time. This need progressively increases and becomes a pattern that can eventually lead to sexual shutdown.

There is another common misperception concerning fulfillment that places limitations on orgasm and the sexual experience itself. This misperception is the assumption that ejaculations are the same as orgasms. On the contrary, **an ejaculation is only a physiological manifestation of a deeper experience and is, for many men, the way to escape or avoid the fuller, loving, sacred, orgasmic experience.**

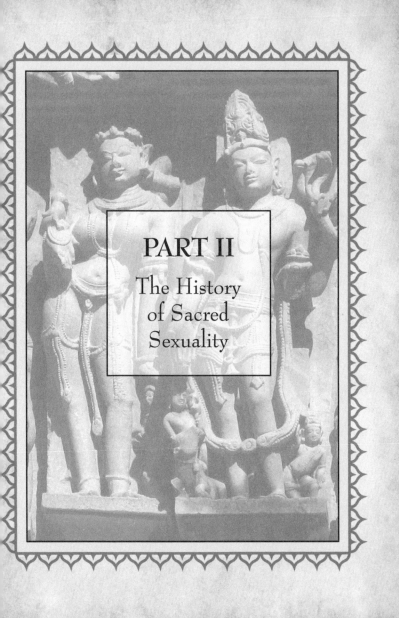

PART II

The History
of Sacred
Sexuality

The Search for Love
It's About Time

*F*or too many years, we have attempted to deny our bodies and have focused on prayer and meditation as our primary means of self-discovery and communion with the Divine. Now, after suffering the fallout from years of sexual abstinence and repression (expressed in the form of the Dark Ages and Inquisitions), we are beginning to understand that **the completion of the soul's journey is proportionate to our ability to integrate spirituality (the heart) *and* sexuality (the body).**

"In Sutra alone (the fundamental teachings of Buddha) there is no liberation. The Highest Yoga Tantra teachings are Buddha's ultimate intention."

—*Mahamudra Tantra (Geshe Kelsang Gyatso)*

After years of sexual confusion and suppression, researchers are substantiating the ancient and modern techniques and beliefs of the practitioners of sacred sexuality. Ironically, most of the wonderful discoveries and insights that modern science has to offer were already known by the ancient practitioners of sacred sexuality.

Ancient Practitioners
of Sacred Sexuality

In the Beginning

*A*lthough humanity has often struggled with sexuality and similar, related issues, there have always been arts and sciences devoted to honoring the sacred, sexual self. In fact, the universe and its origins are steeped in a fusion (or intercourse) of creative forces in cosmic and human forms. All sacred thought systems contain concepts of male and female aspects of this Creative Force. Additionally, every major religion and philosophy has a sect devoted to mysticism. **Each sect of mysticism has a faction devoted to understanding and exploring the deeper concepts behind sacred sexuality and the practical integration of spirituality and sexuality.**

The practice of sacred sexuality dates back to an ancient culture known as the Lemurians. Although there are no known written records of their sexual practices, their methods were kept alive through their descendants, such as the indigenous people of the Hawaiian Islands. The Lemurians combined creativity, vibrational healing, aromatherapy, and spirituality. They lived in harmony with body and soul, and honored the creative and feminine aspects of life. They were also the originators of the healing art known as Reiki, which was preserved by their descendants in Tibet and surrounding regions. All other ancient arts of sacred sexuality are remnants of those founded by this original race.

The oldest arts of sacred sexuality that *have* been preserved in a relatively complete form are those of Tantra and the Taoist arts of sexology, estimated to be several thousand years old. The Western mystics who explored sacred sexuality in the concealed form of alchemy or energetic transmutation came much later. Nevertheless, whatever the name of the sacred art or the time in which it was practiced, the goals have always been the same. The arts of sacred sexuality have always been practiced with the intent of transforming mundane thoughts, feelings, and energy into a higher, spiritualized, personal experience of oneness, or union, with all that exists.

Tantra

Tantra is arguably the oldest known art of sacred sexuality practiced today. The true story of the origins of Tantra is obscure, to say the least. According to legends, Tantra was passed down from spiritual masters who lived in the ancient South Pacific continent of Lemuria that sank beneath the sea, sending survivors to find refuge in Tibet. From this spiritual, vortex-like womb, Tantra was introduced to India and reborn in the form of Hindu and Buddhist Tantra—even though the practice of Tantra is usually deemed unacceptable to the fundamentalists of either of these religions (and most other religions for that matter).

Hindu Tantra integrated the practice of yoga, which like Tantra, focuses on liberation and joining. In fact, many of the physically challenging sexual positions of Tantric lovemaking are actually yoga postures (*asanas*) used for personal awakening.

Tantra is similar to the multileveled system of yoga, for both are like a flower with many petals or a gem with many facets. Tantric *sex* is only one aspect of Tantra. Other facets include the study of sound, visualization, cooking, aromatherapy, and spirituality. One purpose of sexual Tantra is to expand and prolong the physical, energetic, psychological, and spiritual connection between two lovers. Tantric sex brings participants together in such a profound state of oneness and ecstasy that it results in a heightened awareness of the individual practitioner's True Self.

Tantra is a Sanskrit word of two parts. The prefix, *tan*, means "to expand, join, or weave." The latter part, *tra*, means "tool." Therefore, the definition of the term *Tantra* has a twofold meaning—"a tool to expand, liberate, and bring together." The concept of *expansiveness* is one of Tantra's most important precepts. It urges practitioners to push (expand) beyond accepted moral and social limits, judgments, and opinions. In so doing, practitioners demonstrate their beliefs that "There is only God . . . God is only Love and . . . the only rule you should live by is that of sharing love, without limits."

The most advanced writings on Tantra exist in tantric yoga scriptures and in rare Hindu and Buddhist (particularly Tibetan Buddhist) texts referred to as "Tantras." Nevertheless, the most *popular* writings describing the practice of Tantra and sacred sexuality are the *Kama Sutra* (Indian, written by Vatsyayana circa the second century A.D.); followed by the *Ananga Ranga* (Indian, written by Kalyanamalla circa 1200 A.D.); and finally, *The Perfumed Garden* (Arabian, written by Sheikh Nefzaoui circa the sixteenth century A.D.). Ultimately, the purest form of Tantra is not passed down in writing, but only through initiations and personal instruction.

*How delicious an instrument is woman, when
artfully played upon; how capable is she of
producing the most exquisite harmony, of
executing the most complicated variations of love,
and of giving the most divine of erotic pleasures.*

—*Ananga-Ranga*

The *Kama Sutra* was written by a noble man who
viewed life as consisting of *dharma* (spiritual substance),
artha (financial substance), and *kama* (sensual substance).
Kama is said to be "the enjoyment of appropriate objects
by the five senses . . . assisted by the mind, together with
the soul." Thus, the *Kama Sutra* teaches how to attain
and maintain sensual pleasure.

Although Tantra might appear to be an art of sexual
pleasuring and the *Kama Sutra* a manual of sexual
positions, the real goal of *kama* is to cultivate love and
reverence for the person with whom the Tantric experience
is shared. Although pleasure is an attribute of practicing
Tantra, Tantra represents the attainment of love combined
with sensual pleasure.

As practiced in the modern Western world, Tantra often
is a spin-off of the "free love" of the sixties—using body
movement, breathwork, and various forms of stimulation to

achieve higher levels of orgasm or sexuality. Consequently, Tantra is often mistakenly seen as an art geared exclusively toward sexuality. This view is far from accurate. In truth, with genuine Tantra (as with all forms of mysticism) the goal is not about doing or stimulating. Instead, it's about experiencing love without objectification or attachments to a particular person or outcome. Such limitations are seen as constrictions and obstacles to surrendering to Love Absolute.

Although most spiritual disciplines insist that in order to evolve into higher states of consciousness, you must control or deny the senses and lower states of consciousness, Tantra teaches that you cannot experience complete personal and spiritual liberation while restricting any part of your being. Tantra is a profound form of active meditation that expands consciousness using the senses to take you *beyond* the realm of the senses. It teaches that sacred sexuality is a way of deepening intimacy and expanding consciousness, a way to achieve freedom from limitations and to join with the Divine.

*He who knows the truth of the body can
then know the truth of the universe.*

—Rat Nas Tantra

Observing a Tantric experience, you might assume you are simply witnessing "great sex." But if you could see the experience clairvoyantly, you would witness an amazing dance of energy and color, not unlike a fireworks display. Furthermore, if you could see into the hearts and souls of the participants, you would observe a consecrated joining of loving intent.

Valerie Brooks, author of *Tantric Awakening*, summarizes the stages of the Tantric lovemaking experience as follows:

1. *Physical: total concentration on the physical pleasure in the moment.*
2. *Emotional: immersion in loving thoughts and worship of your partner's divinity.*
3. *Spiritual: feeling yourself and your partner as a single unit that is connected to Spirit, or God.*

Just as some of the world's greatest spiritual teachers have said that Heaven cannot be accurately described in words, the essence of Tantra cannot be captured in either oral or written words. **To truly understand Tantra, you have to *experience* it.**

In addition to cosmic, mystical experiences, Tantric masters are also interested in having deeply personal interactions with other people and the world in which they live. When a deep interconnection is established, the formerly perceived space between any two people or objects becomes filled with the light of Spirit. This spiritual presence activates and excites the etheric energy within and between the two, joining them as one. That which was contracted and separate is now free to unite and expand. *This* is Tantra!

Genuine Tantra is a spiritual path and is practiced with the reverence reserved for all things sacred. Since Tantra is a spiritual ceremony, as with all forms of worship, there is an acknowledging and honoring of a Divine Being. In Tantra, this deity is reflected and honored in your partner, rather than as an intellectual concept or vague image. Hence, Tantra is not an abstract form of spiritual practice, but a practical one, wherein the experience with the Divine is brought down to the very realm of the senses. Such an experiential process makes it possible to have the tangible, personal relationship with God that is so often sought but not found. Of course, this is not to say that a Tantrika (practitioner of Tanta) cannot choose to practice other forms of spirituality and worship as well; it's just that Tantra challenges lovers to see the Divine Presence of God in and through *each other*.

Tantra has two distinct, traditional paths of training: a left-hand path (vama-marga) and a right-hand path (dakshina-marga). The left-hand path practices a more liberal form of Tantra that usually interprets literally the ancient teachings of Tantra that refer to intercourse between two lovers. Therefore, this path involves heightened sensuality and sometimes even intercourse. Practitioners of left-hand path Tantra vary from one group to another, with some focusing more on sexuality, others on internal energy development, others on magic, and still others on a blend of the above. Conversely, the right-hand path of Tantra, with its emphasis on spirituality, rather than sexuality, is closer to being an actual religion and is similar to the more traditional religious practices of Buddhism and Hinduism. Rather than seeking a literal sexual experience, the right-hand path of Tantra views intercourse as an allegory of the body mating with Spirit. Therefore, on this path, most of the Tantra rituals and exercises are performed solely within the mind and body of the individual practitioner.

Additionally, there is a third, relatively unknown, and rarely practiced, path we will refer to as "middle-path" Tantra, which is a balanced blend of the previously mentioned left-hand (sexuality) and right-hand (spirituality) paths. This middle-path of Tantra is defined most accurately as being synonymous with authentic forms of "Spiritual Tantra" and/or "Sacred Sexuality." Despite numerous claims to the contrary, most Tantra groups in the Western world are of the left-hand path (focused on sexuality) and are clearly not right-hand path Tantra (focused on spirituality) nor middle-path Tantra (a balanced blend of the two).

In Tantric writings, a woman's sexual and spiritual energies are often referred to as "shakti." In Hindu traditions the goddess Shakti represents the female principle or energy. Although the female force, or shakti, exists in both women and men, women are seen as the "guardians" of the shakti energy. According to ancient Tantric writings, the power of the shakti is limitless. Once awakened, this spiritual, energetic, and sexual force can be channeled creatively.

Upon awakening, Shakti rises up the spine to meet Shiva, her male counterpart. Together their merged energies create an alchemical fusion of bliss. Thus in Tantra, the coupling of a man and woman serves to represent the greater, universal creative process, as the intercourse between a couple simulates the creation dance of Shakti and Shiva.

Despite misrepresentations to the contrary, Tantra is a system of spiritual mysticism *and* personal experience, not exclusively a sexual art. The primary components for practicing *authentic* Tantra include various forms of meditation and kundalini yoga. More specifically, Tantra incorporates *asanas* (yoga postures), *pranayama* (specific breathing techniques), *mantras* (repetition of sacred syllables), *yantras* (visualization), and *bandhas* (muscular energy locks). Just practicing tantric breathing and mind focusing exercises of themselves are very effective in adding to *any* truly sacred experience.

Although Tantra (from India and Tibet) and Taoism (from China) share some similar concepts, the differences are very distinct. For example, Tantra uses more ceremony and ritual, while Taoism is more scientific or methodical and focuses on the body, its meridians, and energy systems. Tantra emphasizes the *art* of sex, while Taoist sexology emphasizes the *science*. In Tantra there is less emphasis on "controlling orgasms" by "constricting specific muscles." Instead, in the art of Tantra there is emphasis on relaxing into the orgasmic sensations, rather than tensing in any form. On the other hand, in the Taoist sexual systems, control and muscle constriction are at the very heart of the techniques and principles.

Taoist Sexology

Although Taoism (pronounced *dow-ism*), as a philosophy or religion in China, developed later than the Hindu religion of India, both traditions embraced some form of sacred sexuality. The Chinese sexual arts were developed by the Yellow Emperor (Huang-Ti) and his "three immortal ladies" long before Taoism, which means that although Hinduism is older than Taoism, the Chinese sexual arts are still as ancient as Tantra.

Like Tantra, Taoism has many facets, sex being only one of eight "spokes to their wheel." Royalty often consulted the wise and respected Taoist masters on issues related to philosophy, health, life, and sex. Some of these teachings were preserved and are known as "Canons of Wisdom." The most common set of ancient writings on Taoist lovemaking is called the "pillow books."

The primary purpose behind Taoist lovemaking is the transformation of sexual energy into healing energy and vitality, resulting in better health and potential immortality. The primary Taoist technique to achieve these healing effects is called the inward orgasm (in-jaculation), whereby the orgasmic energy rises up the spine, stimulating the endocrine glands, energy systems, nervous system, and organs. **Taoists teach that an inner orgasm (in-jaculation) stimulates life and vitality, while the outer orgasm (e-jaculation) brings death or loss of health and vitality.** An in-jaculation is the most effective tool for transforming a physical orgasm into an energetic orgasm. Of course, there are even higher levels of orgasm as well, including a soul-level, total-being orgasm.

In sexual intercourse, semen must be regarded as a most precious substance. By saving it, a man protects his very life. Whenever he does ejaculate, the loss of semen must then be compensated by absorbing the woman essence.

—Peng-Tze *(Secrets of the Jade Bedroom)*

Taoist self-transformation exercises are designed to bring the practitioner to a state of immortality by cultivating what they refer to as the three energies, or "Three Treasures." The first is *ching* (sexual and physical energy), the second is *qi* (etheric and breath energy), and the third is *shen* (mental and spiritual energy). Only with sufficient *ching* can the body produce sufficient *qi*. Then, with sufficient *qi,* a balance of *shen* is restored. These three essences must be restored and refined to their optimum level and balance to attain the gifts of the "Three Treasures," or the "Elixir of Immortality." Practitioners of Taoist sexuality believe that sexual energy is the most powerful human energy and that the use of sexual rejuvenation and in-jaculation techniques are the most effective and efficient way to revitalize and develop these "Three Treasures."

Taoists use imaginative, and sometimes humorous, metaphors to illustrate their concepts about sexuality. For example, they regard man as fire and woman as water. Fire, once started, burns fast and can burn out, while, on the other hand, the woman (or water) is just beginning to boil (or get hot). Therefore, the man must control his fire to prolong his climax (and erection). Then he can help the woman reach her natural stages of warming up toward orgasm, thus enhancing the experience for both partners.

Taoists do not merely teach exercises to enhance the pleasure of partnership. They also encourage self-mastery and self-awareness for improved health and vitality. They clearly teach the importance of drawing in the sexual energy and experience, rather than focusing on sexual organs and external stimuli. Any focus on the sexual organs is used only to introduce the practitioner to more advanced concepts. Taoist master Mantak Chia says that the goal of Taoist sexual practices is like that of making chicken broth: If you boil a chicken in water and extract the vital essence into the water, which is more valuable, the chicken or the broth? Clearly, **the Taoists believe the**

valuable energy generated during lovemaking is more vital to one's well-being than the stimulation to the organs.

Taoists treat sex as a healing art. Since the hands are considered primary channels of energy, they are used in various positions and techniques to assist in lovemaking. For example, during a sexual encounter, the hands (charged with healing energy) are placed over areas that lack vitality or seem to need healing.

Another example of blending the use of healing with sexuality involves recognizing that the partner doing the moving is bringing healing to the partner who is lying (or sitting) still. Since Taoists encourage the awareness and use of healing energy for both partners, **alternating active roles during a sexual encounter is necessarily vital to achieving equal opportunities for healing.**

Sexuality of the Western Mystics

Since the human etheric body is very similar to that of plants, the ancient Native Americans had a ritual that revitalized the human energy field by hugging a tree. The same principle of rejuvenation applies to a child who instinctively rolls around in the grass. Like the Native Americans, the ancient Essenes (an ascetic group of mystics that lived in the Judean region long before, and up until, the time of Christ) also had a ritual whereby they revitalized themselves. They used exercises that would transform their sexual energy into a usable force for growth and well-being. During these rituals they prayed, "Angel of Life, enter my generative organs and regenerate my whole body."

According to some of the Essene manuscripts, **the masters in the Essene community were more apt to achieve transmutation of energy by thought, while the students still used the more physical rituals for stimulation, arousal, and transmutation.**

During the Middle Ages, long after the disappearance of the mystic Essenes, the art of sacred sexuality was known as *alchemy*, meaning "All-Chemistry" or "God's Chemistry." This lost science was said to have been the art of transmuting base metals into gold. It's now understood that the Western mystics were actually using metaphor to discuss their art of sacred sexuality. They were describing the transmutation of base, sexual energy into valuable, ecstatic, soul-level orgasms.

Tales of Sacred Sex

The following are myths, legends, and stories of sacred sexuality from numerous cultures throughout history. Each legend possesses valuable insights into the meaning of sacred sexuality.

ACTAEON AND DIANA

When Actaeon, (a respected hunter who symbolizes the physical self) happened upon the great goddess Diana, naked and washing herself, he failed to fall down and worship her. Instead, he chose to make a sexual advance. Because he failed to see and honor her divinity, she turned him into a stag (symbolizing his out-of-control horniness). Afterwards, Actaeon's own hunting dogs devoured him. This story suggests that when our sexual desires are out of control and we fail to recognize the sacred spirit within that which we desire, our actions will inevitably destroy us.

CUPID AND PSYCHE

The story of Cupid and Psyche offers deep insights into the connection between eroticism and spirituality. Cupid, who is also known as Eros, or Amour, is the god of erotic love, and Psyche represents the beauty of the soul.

When the goddess Venus becomes jealous of Psyche's beauty, Venus asks Eros to cause Psyche to fall in love with some unworthy man. Instead, Eros takes Psyche away to his own secret place, where he protects and visits her under the cloak of darkness, so she never sees his face. Eros explains to Psyche that although he is a god, he doesn't want her to fear or revere him, but to love him as an equal. Herein, the story reveals the importance of mutuality and equality in a relationship of love.

Eventually, Psyche is coaxed by her envious sisters to break her vow to Eros and to attempt to see her lover in the light. So while he is sleeping, she takes a candle to bed to see his face. But the hot wax drips on his shoulder and awakens him. Sadly, Eros flies away on his white wings after telling Psyche, "Love cannot dwell with suspicion." This story conveys the invaluable lesson that trust is necessary if lovers are to remain united. In breaking their agreement to honor the mystery, Psyche attempted to know her lover through her eyes and mind, instead of allowing the *knowing* of her heart to be sufficient. Hence, in her attempt to limit and control Eros, she sacrificed everything.

Later, after Psyche is put through some seemingly impossible initiations by the goddess Venus (tests which Eros secretly helps her pass), the goddess is satisfied and allows Psyche to drink the sacred ambrosia and become immortal. Thus, Psyche is reunited with Eros, and they begin an eternal union.

Eventually, the union of Eros and Psyche (sexuality and spirituality) produces a daughter, whose name is Pleasure, suggesting that true pleasure can be attained only through the proper, healthy union of the loving soul (Psyche) with the passionate body (Eros). Furthermore, for this union to survive, it must be revered as sacred and maintain the elements of spontaneity and mystery.

DIONYSUS—THE GOD OF ABANDON

Although the story of Dionysus might seem unfamiliar, elements of his legend are firmly embedded in modern history, religion, and psychology. Dionysus is the personification of divine ecstasy, which, in human hands, can bring either transcendent joy or madness—spiritual liberation or physical addiction. The word *ecstasy* comes from the root *ex stasis*, meaning "to stand outside oneself" (which is what happens when we have an experience that is too powerful for the body to contain).

Dionysus is often referred to as the god of abandon, the god of ecstasy, or the god of the *vine*, meaning "wine," but not "drunkenness," as often portrayed. In fact, drunkenness was not permitted at ancient Dionysian gatherings, since it was believed that one had to maintain conscious awareness to avoid being possessed by negative spirits while in such a vulnerable and open state.

Dionysus represents the ecstasy of the senses and the sensuous world and is therefore the antithesis of the intellectual thought processes. Ancient civilizations honored Dionysus by many names and in diverse forms. In fact, the practice of the *orgy* was originally a ritual honoring the god Dionysus—the god of liberation and abandon. The theater is also said to have originated as one of the Dionysian rituals.

Since he represented the awakening of the earth, the Christians turned the youthful, androgynous, and beautiful Dionysus into a goat image, depicted with what they perceived as the face of the devil. Yet, paradoxically, many churches still practice Dionysian rituals. In fact, there are numerous parallels between Dionysus and Jesus—making Jesus a living embodiment of Dionysus. Both are sons of Divine Fathers and mortal, virgin mothers. The mothers of both are said to have ascended to Heaven. The father of Dionysus is Zeus (sometimes called *Dias-Pitar*, meaning "God, the father"), while that of Jesus is referred to as "the Father, God." Both beings are said to have visited hell, or the underworld, and both Dionysus and Jesus were hailed as "King of Kings."

Additionally, both Dionysus and Jesus both die and are reborn, becoming symbols of transformation. Afterward, Dionysus ascends to Olympus and Jesus to Heaven, while both sit at the right hand of God. The name *Dionysus* means "son of God," while Jesus was also called the "son of God."

Dionysus and Jesus both suffered at the hands of local authorities and were said to have mingled with men and women of questionable character and low repute. Also, both show a disregard for the established modes of worship.

Given all the similarities between Dionysus and Jesus, it becomes clear that both beings personify the living Christ, one as a mythological archetype and the other as a living incarnation. Dionysus is the male archetype of

Christ consciousness expressed in sensual form just as Mary Magdalene is for the female.

PARADISE LOST

The English poet John Milton reveals incredible insights into the role and higher purpose of sexual encounters. In *Paradise Lost*, he depicts a conversation between Adam and the Archangel Raphael. Here, Adam shares his perplexing attraction for Eve as follows:

> *"To love thou blam'st me not, for love thou say'st*
> *Leads up to heav'n, is both the way and guide;*
> *Bear with me then, if lawful what I ask:*
> *Love not the heav'nly spirits, and how their love*
> *Express they, by looks only, or do they mix*
> *Irradiance, virtual or immediate touch?"*
> *To whom the Angel, with a smile that glowed*
> *Celestial rosy red, love's proper hue,*
> *Answered: "Let it suffice thee that thou know'st*
> *Us happy, and without love no happiness.*
> *Whatever pure thou in the body enjoy'st*
> *(And pure thou wert created) we enjoy*
> *In eminence, and obstacle find none*
> *Of membrane, joint, or limb . . ."*

In this poem, Milton touches upon some of the themes of Genesis Chapters I and II. He implies that it *is* possible for human partnerships to be blessed with love; that the body was created pure; that sexual intercourse is pure and undefiled as long as the soul and body are properly connected to their Divine Source; and that human sexual love is a reflection of a greater Love Divine. Milton also implies that although the angels have a higher vibrational presence, they still enjoy some form of passionate expression. He further indicates that despite the higher form of angelic interaction, the angels themselves do not hold a judgment for the seemingly more limited human expressions through "membranes, joints, or limbs."

SHAKTI AND SHIVA

Shakti and Shiva are female and male Tantric deities representing the masculine and feminine aspects of a greater deity. Although these beings are deified, they are *both* found within all men and women. The whole universe is said to be created from the union of Shakti and Shiva.

In Hindu mythology, Shiva (man) needs Shakti (woman) to give him form, and Shakti (woman) needs Shiva (man) to give her consciousness. He can teach her wonderful things, but she can always humble him by reminding him of his limits. In this sense, the two are necessary to achieve the perfect universal dance of life.

Modern Practices
of Sacred Sex

A New Sexual Paradigm

The he model of *modern* sacred sexuality has the same theme, or goal, as its predecessors, but with two primary differences. First, today's arts of sacred sex are a melting pot, or synthesis, of the more ancient practices. Second, **because of the prevalence of sexual abuse and generations of sexual repression, the future for practicing true sacred sexuality includes a greater emphasis on sexual issues and sexual healing.** This healing is necessary to make room within a person's being for a greater quantity and higher quality of energetic ecstasy.

In an age when people believe that "more is better," it's no wonder men and women obsess over shallow levels of sexual relations and feel pressured to have orgasms, or even multiple orgasms. Yet, people actually need to move in the opposite direction—slow down, relax, and heal the inhibitions, fears, and traumas causing the constrictions that prevent the fullest release and most expansive experience possible. **To experience the most profound levels of sexual ecstasy, the practitioner must be willing to release, even if only temporarily, the drive for explosive orgasms and surrender to a quest for self-discovery and healing.**

Additionally, in modern times, with so much information available on sexuality, there is a growing eclectic approach to sacred sex. People are able to pick and choose the best from all of the ancient arts of sexuality. There is also a growing use of the sexual arts for *healing*, especially for issues like sexual abuse. Consequently, as people heal, they begin to experience themselves and others differently.

The sexual healing process involves learning the difference between healthy (spirit-centered) and unhealthy (ego-centered) sexual encounters. For example, there are numerous characteristics that differentiate an ego-centered encounter from a sacred sexual one. The former involves a search for pleasure and the fulfillment of a sense of lack, while the latter is based on sharing of expansiveness, freedom, and unconditional love. The ego-centered encounter involves judgment, control, and selfish agendas. It's motivated by the need to capture and possess a desired person (or object) who eventually becomes unfulfilling, which leads to the search for yet another person (or object). However, **in a spiritual encounter, all relationships are seen as mirrors of the self, while the heart remains open to freely express and receive love without possessiveness.** This freedom creates a feeling of inner peace and fills the body with trembling vibrations or waves of energy. Ultimately, each new (spiritually focused) sexual encounter is a fresh and loving experience that reflects the presence of the whole universe.

Love is the secret key; it opens the door to the divine. Laugh, love, be alive, dance, sing, become a hollow bamboo and let His song flow through you.

—Osho

Although no single set of guidelines for practicing sacred sexuality is right for everyone, some common principles include the following:

1. Sex is one of the most powerful manifestations of intimacy and love.
2. The most profound experience of sex begins with individual self-awareness and healing.
3. Safety is a crucial part of an intimate, ecstatic experience.

4. Foreplay is an important part of intimacy and should begin with an awareness of your partner's body and needs.

5. Sacred sexuality means paying more attention to prayer, meditation, environment, aromas, music, breathing, clothing, and intimate contact (smiling, kissing, gazing, biting, tickling, and touching).

6. Sex is not the goal in sacred sexuality—love is!

7. Orgasms are not the goal of sacred sex, so relax and enjoy *all* feelings.

8. Sacred sexuality can enhance all sensations, including orgasms.

9. When approaching an orgasm, you can choose to experience various levels of ecstatic release. There are physical orgasms (e-jaculations) and energetic orgasms (in-jaculations), as well as emotional, mental, and soul-level (total-being) orgasms.

Sex Therapy

Most sex therapists are trained counselors specializing in human sexuality and are not sex surrogates, which is another field of sexual healing. Nevertheless, because sex therapy involves a subject with such fear-based stigma, it bears the burden of controversy. For some people, sex therapy can be an invaluable way of accessing and dealing with sexual issues—potentially to a point of resolution.

A sex therapist is also an educator who is usually well informed on the subject of human sexuality. The treatment routine varies from person to person but generally includes education concerning human sexuality, as well as specific sexual exercises recommended as homework. The education and exercises are prescribed to the client and partner (if applicable) to help them reprogram their minds and bodies concerning the subject of sexuality.

Sex therapy is often sought out by individuals who suffer from such forms of sexual dysfunction as addiction and inhibitions. It is also sought out to resolve sexual issues between partners. The most common themes addressed in sex therapy are the lack of sexual arousal, the inability to reach orgasm, and the inability to orgasm during intercourse. The treatment routine often includes working on relationship issues, as well as learning various sexual techniques. Progressive forms of sex therapy are very effective and usually reap positive results.

Sexual Healing

As previously mentioned, sexual therapy is a valid technique for healing sexually related issues. However, it is but the first in at least three forms of *sexual healing*.

All forms of sexual healing are effective for balancing and healing the "root chakra" or pelvic region—areas that often hold sexual shame. Yet, despite the success of all types of sexual healing, some styles (such as sex surrogates) are still frowned upon by even the most "open-minded" healers and therapists. Therefore, getting hands-on assistance with these kinds of issues is relatively difficult, since there are very few therapists who are trained in this field and are willing to risk entering the realm of one of humanity's greatest taboos.

In most cases, there are three phases of sexual healing, which should follow this order:

1. **Sex Therapy** (counseling)
2. **Contact Therapy** (hands-on)
3. **Sacred Sexuality** (such as Tantra).

As mentioned, the most widely accepted form of sexual healing is the *first phase—sex therapy*—that actually resembles counseling and psychotherapy and mostly involves conversation, exercises, and homework related to the client's particular sexual issues. If there is any concern about potential sexual issues, inhibitions, and/or abuse, the counseling phase should be experienced first before moving into the second, or contact phase, which might include physical bodywork, sensual massage, and even exercises in arousal.

The *second phase* of sexual healing is a more radical stage, which includes the hands-on approach of *sex surrogates*. Sex surrogates are usually not licensed and are rarely acknowledged and accepted by the more mainstream professionals. Nevertheless, they play a potentially valid role in the goal of sexual healing. A trained *sex therapist* might verbally teach a man who suffers from premature ejaculation how to deal with the fears that lead to this problem. A *sexual surrogate*, on the other hand, might work with a man who suffers from premature ejaculation and show him how to prevent this problem by learning specific techniques while having sex with the therapist or surrogate. Both systems are valuable and effective, but merely take different approaches.

The *third phase* of sexual healing is the practice of some type of *sacred sexuality*. Although many individuals might prefer to jump right into the third form of sexual healing (the blissful phase arising from having done thorough work in the other two stages), it's best to experience the initial two stages of sexual healing first. The initial steps of healing should reveal any personal issues concerning sexuality that need to be addressed, which, if ignored, could trigger greater trauma.

Ultimately, if a person can find the courage to walk through the gauntlet of sexual healing, the rewards are countless and far-reaching. While the time it takes to heal varies for each person, **the ultimate goal for us all is to experience and integrate: (1) a union with God; (2) a union within our own being (mind, body, and soul); and (3) potentially a union with partners.**

Sexual healing can assist to release trauma, restore normal sexual functions, and release unhealthy inhibitions and shame. It can also encourage self-esteem and awaken unconditional love and self-worth—physically, emotionally, mentally, and spiritually. As we individually heal these restricting issues, we do so for all humanity.

The Role of a Sexual Partner, Healer, or Therapist

Who *facilitates* sexual healing? There are counselors who specialize in this field, as well as individuals who have studied the arts of sacred sexuality. The latter group has much to offer, but a background in the psychology of trauma is highly recommended. Additionally, a friend or partner can learn some of the exercises to assist in facilitating the healing process.

There are, nonetheless, some hazards and potential pitfalls in having a friend or partner acting as the healer, rather than a therapist. If things go well, the healer often becomes the object of "transference." In this case, the client believes his or her newfound awakening is inseparably attached to the healer. On the other hand, if deep wounds are awakened, and a friend or partner is assisting the healing process, then the recipient of sexual therapy might "project" some of the hurt and rage onto the loved one. This, of course, could ruin their relationship.

It is also possible to have a mixture of transference and projection.

There are precautions that can be taken to avoid the inherent pitfalls of sexual therapy. Yet, with such a taboo subject embodying so many deep issues, there are no guarantees of avoiding transference and projection. In fact, in the practice of Tantra, it's often expected that a student *will* become attracted (if not attached) to the teacher. This attraction is seen as a natural part of a student's awakening process. If treated responsibly by both parties, it can become a valuable tool to deepen their mutual vulnerability and trust.

For sexuality to reach a level worthy of being called sacred, it takes the cooperation of healthy and aware partners and healers. This healthy attitude includes unconditional love together with the willingness to develop specific skills and learn the necessary exercises for their roles as partners, healers, or therapists. Last, but not least, for partners or healers to be truly effective, they must have clear boundaries and their personal needs and issues healed (or in the process of healing).

THINGS A PARTNER OR SEXUAL HEALER SHOULD AVOID

1. Making sex (in any form) the goal of encounters.
2. Making orgasms the goal of sexual encounters.
3. Ignoring the needs of a partner or client.
4. Ignoring the issues, inhibitions, and tensions of a partner or client.
5. Disconnecting or losing the ability to remain present with a partner or client.

The Future of Sacred Sexuality

As humanity moves beyond the dogmas and stigmas that keep people imprisoned in a fear-based past, especially regarding sex, the human race will obtain a level of freedom rarely imagined. This vision of responsible love and uninhibited freedom will one day manifest for all people. This vision is at the heart of all religions and philosophies—even if they do not yet realize it. They all have the same underlying goal of returning to the All. The major difference between these various thought systems, however, is the form the journey takes. Nevertheless, out of this journey will arise a world of greater acceptance, one that honors and embraces the sacredness in all things—including sexuality.

You don't have to spiritualize sex to make it valuable, because by its very nature sex is a deep act of the interior life and always brings with it a wealth of emotional and spiritual meaning.

—Thomas Moore

PART III

Self
Awareness

Know Thyself

Getting to Know You

$\mathcal{S}$elf-awareness means just that—you are aware of, and can focus on, *yourself*. You give top priority to the physical, energetic, emotional, mental, soul-level, and spiritual aspects of your being. Furthermore, you take responsibility for your own safety and growth.

To love oneself is the beginning of a life-long romance.

—Oscar Wilde

Although the question concerning how to find the "perfect partner" is often raised, the answer lies in loving and respecting *yourself*—first. As you heal your issues and become *healthier*, you'll feel *happier* and more *attractive*. **When you feel good about yourself, it sends out positive**

"vibes" that are appealing to healthier partners. Then, if and when you *do* choose to relate with another, you'll have a much better chance of developing a rewarding relationship from a solid foundation.

As you get to know yourself, you will discover personal, preconceived beliefs about love, romance, and sex. Whether conscious or not, these preconceptions definitely have an effect on your existing relationships and on those you will attract in the future. Consequently, without the necessary self-awareness, healing, and growth, **changing relationships can be like changing places of residence. You always end up having more "stuff" than you thought.**

You can never truly give to another that which you have not accepted for yourself. So, the ability to fully give your body to a partner in sexual intimacy depends upon your ability to completely accept *your* body. In other words, if you want your partner to accept your body, you must *first* accept it yourself. You must also see yourself as loveable and worthy of acceptance.

If you don't have love for yourself,
you can't be loving to others.

—Dr. Wayne Dyer

The Effects of
Your First Sexual Experiences

The emotional effects of our earliest sexual experiences are so powerful that left unconscious and/or unhealed (where healing is needed), they permanently impact our future sexual choices. A few of these are conscious, but many are not. In many respects, our earliest sexual experiences remain with us for the rest of our lives. For some, the first sexual experience was loving, romantic, and/or educational. For others, the encounter was vastly different. Whether positive or negative, these early events experienced as children, teenagers, or adults determine what our relationships will become. They affect our ability to choose healthy, responsible partners. Nevertheless, whatever unhealthy patterns may have driven us in the past, sexual healing is possible and will assist in the breaking of these patterns that "the experts" predict will remain with us permanently.

Responsibility and Boundaries

Emotions are an important bridge between the physical and spiritual worlds, as well as between physical and soul-level (total-being) orgasms. The unresolved issues within your emotional being need not be healed and perfect, but they certainly must be in the process of *healing*. If left unchecked, your unhealed emotional wounds will act as a barrier to *safety*. Without a feeling of safety, you cannot *trust* totally. Without trust, you cannot experience sacred sexuality and the total-being orgasms that are an integral part of any sacred sexual experience.

If you desire the most amazing sexual experience possible, you need to accept responsibility for creating a safe and tangible connection with God, yourself, and others. You also need to be responsible for doing personal healing work because this work will enable you to create healthier boundaries in your life and with your lovers. **Having clear boundaries means that you are in touch enough with the healthy, loving part of yourself to know what does and doesn't work for your higher good and to choose accordingly.** To establish clear boundaries successfully and consistently requires a sense of self-love and self-worth. As you develop a clearer sense of responsibility and boundaries, you will increase your ability to create relationships wherein you feel enough trust and comfort to openly communicate and heal all that would otherwise keep you from experiencing a life of passion and bliss.

Dealing with Inhibitions

Some people have very serious, justifiable reasons for their sexual inhibitions. Nevertheless, repression of their sexuality is not their natural state of being, nor is it meant to be permanent. With enough courage, anyone and everyone can heal. Healing sexual inhibitions requires pushing through personal issues in this area.

Most of our inhibitions and belief systems (especially those unconsciously chosen) come from our parents, friends, culture, religion, and past experiences. They rarely arise from conscious, clear decisions in the present moment, but instead arise from old, learned patterns. Of course, this conditioning can change if we do a self-inventory and begin a healing process. We are then free to adopt our own opinions—those based on current feelings and inspirations. This freedom gradually results in our letting go and allowing our "true self" to come to life and playfully express the feelings of our hearts.

Healing Sexual Trauma

What is sexual trauma? How do you know if the term applies to you? For people who have been raped or molested, the answers to these questions are usually obvious. However, **sexual trauma can also include being shamed, having abortions, repressing guilt about past sexual behavior, and feeling conflict over religious, social, or family beliefs or ethics.** Basically, any experience that lacks love's presence is traumatic to the heart and soul and therefore affects your life and body.

Sexual trauma results in feelings and memories becoming trapped in the body and causing sexual dysfunction. Traumas or inhibitions can block the neurotransmitters from the genitals to the brain—even to the point, for example, where a woman can physically experience vaginal contractions that simulate an orgasm, *but* her brain receives no signals of pleasure. In such instances, sexual healing techniques can effect a reprogramming of some of these blocked channels. Once new levels of love and trust are imprinted, the woman's yoni can respond with deeper levels of release and orgasm. When healing takes place, the woman's pleasure-signals can move unimpeded to her brain, enabling her to orgasm more easily.

Additionally, trauma and inhibitions can show up as an ability to reach orgasm or even a loss of sensation in the yoni (for a woman) or some forms of erectile dysfunction, impotence, or premature ejaculation (for a man). Successful healing can be assisted, in some cases, by massaging the wounded (numb or painful) region with a slow, light, healing touch, while the recipient breathes as deeply and calmly as possible and remains present.

When your partner is sexually wounded and you are encouraging healing, you are, in effect, asking her (or him) to surrender to a level of trust and freedom that might be new to her. For this reason, it is imperative to gain your partner's trust. **You can earn trust by demonstrating that**

your partner's well-being, and not just the activity of sex, is your primary goal. You can also gain trust by being in tune with your partner—body and soul.

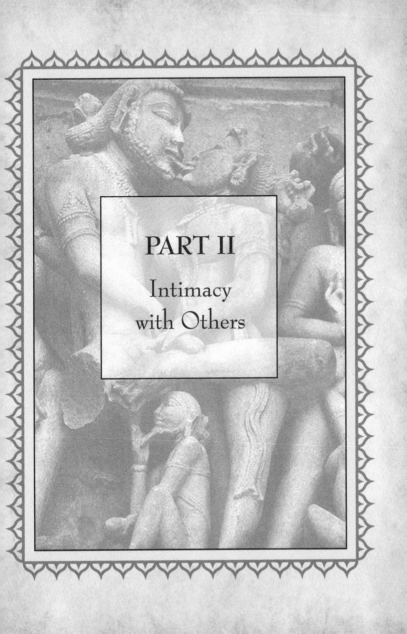

PART II

Intimacy
with Others

Foreplay

Preparing for Love

$\mathcal{F}$oreplay is, as the word implies, play-fullness before intercourse. Therefore, it should be experienced as such—fun and spontaneous, yet enhanced by tools and techniques to stimulate arousal. Foreplay can be a sensual, sexual experience in and of itself, without necessarily progressing to intercourse, but should nearly always be a part of any sexual encounter. Remember, though, that the deep *connection* between partners, more than technique, is the greatest aphrodisiac. So maintain a connection to your own heart and soul with the intent of remaining connected to your partner's heart and soul as well. Be sure to draw from imagination and spontaneity as the foundation for your tools of foreplay. But, most important, take your time. Foreplay, in general, should be slow and lighthearted, rather than rushed or excessively stimulating. If you rush and overstimulate a man, he can suffer premature ejaculation. Overstimulating a woman can result in excessive excitation in her clitoris or G-spot, thus preventing the relaxation necessary for the deepest levels of orgasm.

Love is my ointment, my lubrication, my wetness that wells from deep inside me. Love keeps the body young, the joints oiled. Love is the tingling up the spine, to the neck, into the head. Love is soft. Love is forever. Love is the sunrise and sunset that continue infinitely. Love is the only constant, the indistinguishable. Love is the beginning, and love will be the end. Love is why I am here.

—Valerie Brooks *(Tantric Awakening)*

Playful teasing is an invaluable part of foreplay. Teasing involves enticing your partner onward, offering suggestions of promised delights that draw him or her closer, and then easing off slightly. Effective teasing requires an awareness of the energy level between you and your partner, noticing when the optimum sensations have been reached and then knowing when it is time to back off. Teasing is not a means of controlling your partner, nor is it meant to deny your partner pleasure. Instead, teasing is a means of heightening your partner's arousal and intensifying his or her sensual enjoyment.

Traditionally, the Tantric ritual for lovers begins with the partners symbolically purifying their bodies by washing or bathing each other. Next, lovers connect heart-to-heart by breathing together and exchanging kind words. Then, they connect soul-to-soul by praying together. In addition to the rituals of cleansing and connecting, lovers have many other activities to choose from during their initial stages of lovemaking. The repertoire of foreplay is far greater than genital stimulation in preparation for intercourse. The choices can include any combination of the following:

1. Creating the Environment
2. Cleansing
3. Communicating and Connecting
4. Kissing and Mouth-play
5. Massaging and Caressing
6. Oral Sex

Creating the Environment

Before a sacred sexual encounter, prepare the room that will become your love chamber. Place any necessary supplies close-by *before* you get started, so there will be fewer distractions and less effort for you and your lover, allowing a fuller surrender to the sensations of the moment. Advanced preparation also includes having an empty stomach, colon, and bladder.

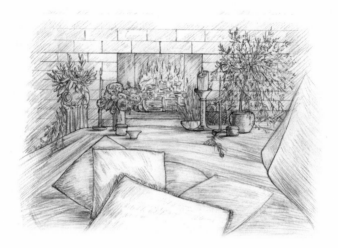

*This sacred space we create enhances the mood.
It heats up my body, and I feel like I am in
a trance. I can close my eyes and a blissful,
dreamlike state washes over me—not sleeping,
not awake. I forget all my problems and flaws
and dive into this idyllic dream of sweat and
wetness that is too good to believe.*

—Valerie Brooks *(Tantric Awakening)*

The undressing of yourself, or each other, can be done at any time during the initial stages of foreplay. Undressing might be included in the early stage of "creating the environment" or during a later part of foreplay, such as "massaging and connecting." **Whenever you choose to unbutton your partner's shirt or blouse or remove his or her pants, remember that you are symbolically disrobing your partner's defenses and exposing the soul.**

Cleansing

For the sake and safety of cleanliness and good hygiene, make bathing or showering together a major part of foreplay. Such cleansings offer an opportunity to introduce bath gels or essential oils. The resulting scent and feeling of being clean and fresh are wonderful, soothing aphrodisiacs.

Cleaning and preparing the body for lovemaking can be seen as acts of self-love arising from a sense of self-worth. Such care and preparation are also statements about the importance of your lover. The ancients were detailed in their descriptions of how to wash and perfume the body. They considered washing to be symbolic of self-purification—not unlike a baptism. Aside from the symbolism of *cleansing*, washing each other's body provides quality, physical contact. In so doing, lovers become more intimately aware of each other's anatomy. Besides, lightly scented, slippery skin feels wonderful.

Communicating and Connecting

Communication, especially about rules and intent, is vital for any intimate relationship or encounter. In fact, communication is *so* important that, for partners who are just getting to know each other, it's even more crucial than the usual initial part of foreplay—"setting the environment." Good communication also assists in creating an even better mood and environment. **Clarity of intent is required within *you* before you can share your intentions with friends and selected lovers.**

When I am . . . able to share what I am truly feeling, my entire body and breath come alive. My body responds to my courage and the truth, it vibrates, it pulsates, it trembles. This makes me . . . realize that I am not really being vulnerable to another but rather to myself.

—Diana Richardson *(The Heart of Tantric Sex)*

Communicating to maintain or increase arousal is a natural progression from communicating needs. It involves using dialog to turn each other on and to stay turned on. However, communication also goes beyond dialog. It includes using sounds, such as moans, to express what feels good and what you want more of. You can use erotic dialog to arouse your lover. It turns your lover on and breaks down his or her resistance and inhibitions. Also, telling your lover that you are aware of what he or she wants and how badly it's wanted allows your lover to feel and crave it more deeply.

The more you communicate with the partner you are pleasuring, the more willing he or she will be to surrender. You earn your partner's trust partly through your confidence, skill, attention, creativity, and clear intent.

It's up to you to get what you want from your lover. Other than communicating needs, the person being pleasured should do very little, except for relaxing and letting go. Although communication skills come into play even before you make physical contact, their importance continues throughout an encounter—until, of course, the two partners no longer need words to communicate. Up to that point, each partner should personally demonstrate to the other how and where he or she would like to be touched, with how much pressure, and for how long. Learning to sense when to add stimulation and when to back off makes you a better lover *and* a better person.

When communicating, be sure to let your partner know how well he or she is doing. You can also tactfully ask your partner to alter or fine-tune what he or she is doing. Let your partner know if these alterations increase arousal. Also be sure to continue giving acknowledgment throughout intimate contact and sexual experiences. That way, your partner knows exactly how he or she is doing and how you are feeling. Acknowledgement or feedback not only acts as a turn-on and makes both partners feel better, it also keeps both of them present and focused.

Sexually arouse your lover by saying what you intend to do to his or her body. In so doing, you bring your lover's attention to it, as well as your own. Tell your lover that you can feel him or her wanting more and that you're going to bring satisfaction if he or she will show you how badly it's wanted. Point out, or acknowledge, to your partner, every time you hear a moan or when you feel subtle things like heat or moisture coming from his or her genitals. This interaction will turn on both of you, while opening up a deeper level of communication. As your lover *asks* for more, he or she opens up to *feeling* more.

There are two ways to become synchronized with your partner: by learning to recognize signs of pleasure in your partner *and* by asking what he or she would like you to do to intensify that pleasure. **The more you focus on the pleasure of your partner, the greater will be your ability to expand and intensify that pleasure.**

Kissing and Mouth-play

Before your mouth ever makes contact with your lover's, your breath can be conveying messages of desire and sensuality. Each in-breath can be a method of drawing in the essence of your lover. Similar to how your eyes widen when you see something wonderful or you inhale deeply when you smell something pleasant, your in-breath suggests you can "taste" your lover from several inches away. Your out-breath sends a message to your lover that you are on the way and getting closer by the second. In practice, this might feel as though you are lightly sucking in air and gently blowing it out. Breathing in and out in this sensuous fashion, while focusing on your lover's response, will arouse wonderful sensations. You can choose to play with the less responsive areas of the body to evoke a greater awareness there, or you can target the obviously pleasurable areas and drive your lover wild.

Most people consider the lips to be an erogenous zone that is responsive as well as capable of evoking a response. The upper lip is considered by Tantrists to be a special erogenous zone for a woman, since it has an invisible channel, or meridian, linking it directly to the clitoris. Notice how common it is for advertisers to use the image of a woman licking her upper lip and how seductive this image appears. The same is true for the lower lip of a man.

Kissing is a highly sensual experience for the body and soul. The forms and styles of kissing range from a simple, quick peck on the lips or cheek to the deepest passionate exchange. Tantric masters refer to kissing as the "meeting of the upper gates." Contact between the genitals is the "meeting of the lower gates." These "gates" designate the opening where an inward and outward exchange, or transfer, of energy takes place.

THE KISS

One Woman's Experience with a Sacred Kiss

One day I asked a man, a teacher of sacred sexuality, if he would be willing to meet me at a cafe for some tea and to answer a few questions about himself and his work. He agreed and we spent an hour talking. He generously answered my many questions. He explained that sacred sexuality is mainly the sharing between souls with an intention of love, safety, respect, and sensuality and that when we are in the space of true, spiritual love (which can also manifest as a sacred sexual encounter), miraculous things can occur—even physiological things. He explained to me that a truly sacred encounter can warp time and evoke healing. I marveled at his words, even though I secretly thought he was clearly exaggerating.

He eventually said that he could see how incredibly nervous I was, so I explained that I had not been alone with a man for quite some time. I even confessed that it was my friends who had convinced me to muster up the courage to invite him to spend a moment with me. So he reassured me, made me laugh at myself, took me on a short walk, and then escorted me to my car, where he surprised me by extending a simple goodnight kiss on my cheek. His kiss expressed so much . . . it said, "Goodnight, thanks for hanging out, it was nice to meet you" . . . all so kind but "matter-of-fact." Nevertheless, it felt so warm and was ever so appreciated. That kiss was exactly what I needed . . . not too much, nor too little.

Then, it happened. I turned to unlock my car and verbalized something similar to what his kiss expressed . . . "Thanks so much for the time. I really appreciate it. Have a great week." And we both smiled and nodded. But then he walked back toward me, placed his warm hands on each side of my face, tilted my head back slightly to look into my eyes and said, "Please remember you are a wonderful being and are ready to dance the 'dance of life' again with a safe partner and/or friends." I responded with a smile and a "thank you." Then he asked if he could give me another kiss goodnight, to which I said, "Yes."

He drew me close against his strong body, gently placed his lips against mine, and held them there for a while with no movement whatsoever. I thought, "Oh, this is a nice surprise, a simple mouth to mouth kiss." But he continued to hold his lips there. For how long, I do not know. Was it seconds or hours? I had no idea, as time melted away, just as he said it would. Although there didn't seem to be any movement, I suddenly realized that my upper lip had shifted to rest between his warm, soft lips.

My lip was resting between his, melting, or was it being dissolved? I became nervous and excited at the same time. I felt a rush of warm energy move gently from my lip to my throat and down to my heart and breasts, all of which seemed to expand. The energy continued down through my tummy until it reached my genitals, which created what I could only describe as a quickening. Now I was feeling more sensual than I ever had, and yet it was different . . . it wasn't lustful. The sensation actually made me jump slightly, which embarrassed me somewhat.

I realized, however, that he wasn't giving any power to my self-doubts or embarrassment. He remained just "being" with the kiss, and with me. This allowed me to quickly return to surrendering, but now even more so.

My whole body melted into his ecstatic kiss. Before I realized it, and without knowing if he would approve, my mouth opened and invited his to do the same. Our lips and tongues began to dance together in perfect motion. They swirled, sucked, and licked as if they were in love with each other.

The kiss may have lasted merely a minute or two. But it seemed timeless, as if it had been hours—for how could so much happen in just a few moments?

Even when the kiss was over, it didn't end. Sensations of warmth, tingling, and life-force continued washing over and through me. My legs were wobbling, and I could feel my body rocking from side to side. Thank goodness he was holding me up.

Then he gently moved away, with his comforting hands being the last to break contact. But before they did, he smiled and thanked me. HE thanked ME! We shared a few more words, and then he suggested that I take great care of myself.

As he walked away, I somehow managed to pour myself into my car and just sat there for a long time. I was basking in thought, sensation, and feeling. When I calmed down enough, without conscious effort, words came out of my mouth, "My friends will never believe this."

Days later, when I was once again reveling in the memory of that kiss, I realized he had given me a real-life demonstration of sacred sexuality. What I had experienced was love, safety, respect, and sensuality. But even more, it was timeless, healing, and miraculous just as he said it could be. But how? It was just a kiss . . . or was it? How could just a kiss feel more complete than any sexual experience I had ever had? Never before had I experienced such a pure and perfect moment, a moment that is still having positive, irreplaceable effects on me—even many months later.

Massaging and Manually Stimulating

It is believed that the skin is the message gatherer for the brain. The body is completely covered by sensitive skin that has millions of sensors capable of sending whispers of pleasure to the brain. Therefore, the entire body is an erogenous zone that is highly responsive to touch. When a person yearns to be touched, it surfaces in the body as something called tumescence. Tumescence awakens slight pulsing contractions of muscles in the body and quickens the various endocrine glands.

The ancient practitioners of sacred sexuality taught five *forms* of physical touch: stroking, pinching, scratching, tapping, and squeezing. Each of these can vary in combination, speed, and pressure. Also, in the art or practice of sacred sexuality, there are three *levels,* or depths, of touching and contact:

1. Massaging touch–contacts the body's tissues at various depths.
2. Internal touch–penetrates a body with the fingers, hands, tongue, and penis.
3. Energetic touch–has no *physical* contact with the body, but still evokes a response.

The proper technique for manually pleasuring (masturbating) another involves far more than the quick and heavy-handed practices of the clumsy learning stages that some people never outgrow. This is not to say that manual stimulation must always be in your love chamber or that it must always be given an hour to accomplish. There is certainly something to be said about spontaneous pleasuring or intercourse in the form of a playful "quickie." However, time should also be provided for lengthier sessions, which offer results that a quickie could never match.

The most powerful forms of manually pleasuring another person to orgasm require an extended amount of attention on the person with whom you are working. If done well, **hand stimulating another person is an art form in itself**. For example, a woman should touch a penis in a fashion that communicates she has found a "pot of gold." Her touch should demonstrate that the act of stimulating her lover's penis arouses *her* as well. The same principle applies to a man making contact with a woman's yoni. Unfortunately, most often a man touches a woman's yoni with a desire to follow through to intercourse or to prove his sexual skills at stimulating his lover. Instead, he should take his time and attentively touch all sections of his lover's yoni with his hands, conveying the message that each part gives him pleasure. A good way to discover the kind of strokes your partner likes is to ask if you may watch him or her do self-pleasuring, so you can learn from what your partner does. Your partner can also take your hand and guide you through his or her favorite technique.

Increase the pleasuring experience by learning how to bring your partner up to an ecstatic peak (without cumming) and then down slightly, only to repeat the process again and again. **The best tools for enhancing pleasure are a loving, caring heart, knowledge of proper pleasuring techniques, and intuitive instincts.** Another effective tool for enhancing pleasure involves the ability to alter the sexual experience through conscious intention—the "power of the mind."

Oral Sex

Although oral sex is considered taboo by some, the ancients taught that oral sex is a delightful addition to any sexual experience. **When practiced correctly, oral sex can be *at least* as pleasurable as intercourse itself.** In the arts of sacred sex, there are several recommended techniques for orally pleasuring a man or a woman. Like mouth kissing, oral sex has numerous variations. It can be experienced as a part of foreplay or complete in itself. Oral pleasuring is a wonderful gift from one person to another or as a simultaneous exchange.

Despite the taboos, there are rewarding aspects to oral pleasuring and ejaculation ingestion. For example, the fluids ejaculated by a male (which average one teaspoon) are high in protein, life-promoting energy, antibiotic properties, and nutrients, including vitamin C, iron, and calcium. Semen, therefore, can be healthy to ingest. Since these nutrients come from the man's body, however, each ejaculation depletes his endocrine glands unless proper techniques are utilized to magnify and retain the otherwise lost vital essence and nutrients.

Before engaging in oral sex, it is advisable that the genitals be as clean as possible and "protection" be considered. Also, the partner pleasuring should have a clean mouth. Cleanliness cuts down on the number of potential germs being transferred. You might use a dental dam (available in flavors) or kitchen cellophane. Of course, these germs become less of a concern if you and your partner have a long-term, monogamous relationship.

Intercourse

The Dance of the Divine

*O*nce lovers have experienced the different stages of love, energy development, and passion by exploring the variations of pleasuring (presented in the previous section of this book), they might choose to move their foreplay into intercourse. Or they might choose to let the previous explorations be sufficient for the moment without moving on to actual penetration. This decision is usually agreed upon in advance but is sometimes made *during* the intimate encounter. Either way, if the choice is made to have intercourse, there are numerous exercises and techniques to enhance this experience.

As with the previously mentioned forms of intimacy and stimulation, it's essential to maintain connection and sensitivity. **Good lovers are keenly aware of their partners.** They know their partners' stages of arousal and are able to read what's going on inside of them—physically, energetically, emotionally, mentally, and spiritually.

Although this may sound like a difficult task, it becomes relatively easy when lovers are sensitive and *care enough* about each other.

If you don't know the way of intercourse,
partaking of herbs (aphrodisiacs) is of no benefit.

—P'eng Tsu

When making love, forget about orgasms. Just make love. Do it slowly enough to feel each sensation and emotion. Taking your time can result in making love for longer periods, which is certainly a great way to deepen the connection in a relationship. Avoid tensing in anticipation of an approaching orgasm, and instead, relax, focus on sharing love, and meld into each other. In fact, let go of *any* goals or agendas and of all unnecessary thoughts. **"Mindless lovemaking" is far more powerful than "mindless sex."**

Being Present

Being fully aware of the present moment is one of the most effective ways to access the soul. When experiencing sacred sexuality, you can increase desire and pleasure by anticipating each stroke from your lover. It is important to appreciate and respond to any degree of sensation, no matter how slight. Be conscious of each stroke, movement, sound or fragrance—every sensation of the moment—to access your soul and that of your lover.

My true self is blossoming. Not by direction or force, just by surrender. And now my sexuality and heart are becoming so merged that I can hardly put my attention on one without exciting the other.

—Valerie Brooks *(Tantric Awakening)*

When making love, you might be thinking about something else—sexual agendas or something totally unrelated to the present experience. To avoid such distractions, remain focused and feel each sensation, as well as the pleasure you are giving and receiving. If, while making love, you start thinking about performance and its result (rather than being in the present moment), focus on one of the techniques for enhancing the sexual experience to help you return to the present. Once refocused in the moment, forget the techniques. Relax, breathe slowly and gently; go with the natural flow of energy as it unfolds. **You need not force anything. Don't be goal-oriented!**

Be in the here and now, and feel every sensation, touch, and subtle movement. Furthermore, the receiving partner should surrender body and soul and remain focused on all orgasmic sensations commencing with (or even before) the first stroke. In other words, the receiving partner should totally yield to his or her partner and surrender to the pleasure being given.

Choosing a Partner

For some people, the concept of having a choice of the person or persons with whom to share intimacy is a novel idea. Nevertheless, not only do you have a choice, but on some level, you have always been involved in creating your partners (or their manifestation into your life). As you learn and evolve, you develop and demonstrate more self-love and self-worth. You then find that your healthier, more confident state of mind has a dramatic effect on the quality of people you attract into your life and with whom you choose to share deeper intimacy.

If, on the other hand, you are already in a relationship, you probably experience one (or a combination) of the following types.

1. Your partner is on the same path and *is* willing to share concepts such as sacred sexuality.

2. Your partner is open to *limited* exploration.

3. Your partner is *not* open to exploring greater forms of true lovemaking.

The last category is unfortunately the most common and creates problems that are not easily solved. Emotionally and spiritually mature practitioners of sacred sexuality, however, never have a shortage of intimate friends and/or potential lovers. There are always wonderful people with whom you can share affection, not necessarily sexually, as in this evolving state of maturity, you are never irresponsibly promiscuous.

In sacred sexuality, the concept of *growing* relationships (from friendships to life-mates) is honored as a responsible means of assuring the most evolved partnerships. Yet, there is a point in your spiritual evolution where you can love someone immediately. This ability to share *immediate* love does not replace the value of growing a relationship over time. Nevertheless, there comes a stage in development where the true love of the soul can be shared with anyone, at any time, and in any form.

When sharing sacred sexuality, there are several different types of relationships from which to choose. They are as follows:

1. **Mutual Using**–occurs when two mature, emotionally healthy, consenting adults agree that they will share sexually; yet they are merely borrowing each other momentarily (and with no attachments) for the purpose of

the experience. This is commonly referred to as "mutual usery." They are not necessarily friends, but they are choosing to be lovers (once or a hundred times). Again, there are no attachments or agendas.

2. **Intimate Friendships**–are relationships that have all the traits of a good friendship, such as honesty, good communication, playfulness, and longevity. However, the friends involved have decided to trust each other with occasional intimacy as well, which can take many forms, ranging from holding each other to full-on sexual intercourse.

3. **Monogamous Partnering**–is, of course, the committed, intimate relationship between two people. The partners have agreed to be faithful to each other. They may be trying out such an arrangement on a short-term basis or they may be life-mates.

4. **Multiple Partners**–is best practiced by only the most responsible individuals. Having more than one lover can easily be an unconscious cover for issues ranging from a lack of commitment to sexual addiction. Therefore, people who choose this experience need to undergo a thorough self-inventory to understand their motivations and assure they are honorable. People with numerous lovers must be honest with themselves and all other parties concerned about their choice of lifestyle. A person with multiple lovers must also practice the safest sex possible.

5. **The Sacred Sexual Relationship**–varies greatly from person to person and couple to couple. Furthermore, a sacred sexual relationship can apply in any of the above definitions, as well as a combination of most of the above.

Sexual Positions

Once lovers have decided to share intercourse, they can let nature takes its course and gradually discover which positions feel best to them. Or they can playfully explore the various positions defined by the arts of sacred sexuality. In either case, the movement from one position to another should be as fluid, effortless, and natural as possible.

Although sacred sexual practices are not about performing sexual calisthenics and having intercourse in as many positions as possible, it *is* advisable to playfully explore several positions during most of your lovemaking experiences. Every system of sacred sexuality has numerous suggested positions for lovemaking. For the purpose of simplicity, they can be grouped into five basic sets: man on top, woman on top, lying on sides, man from behind, and miscellaneous. The last category includes positions that do not fit into the first four groups: for example, when neither person is "on top" (such as standing positions) nor are they both "lying on their sides" (such as when both lovers lie on their backs).

Once again, sexual positions are essentially yoga postures adapted to the art of lovemaking. These positions are good for the health and healing of both partners and are effective for creating energy circuits between lovers. The different angles of penetration stimulate healing to various parts of the body, including organs and glands. Furthermore, the variations, when done with intensity and passion, become an effective cardiovascular exercise. Or, when done slowly and tenderly, they provide numerous opportunities for creating a deeper, soul-level connection between lovers.

Intercourse for Healing

All trauma seeks a home or hideout somewhere in the body. When it does so, it wraps itself in muscle tissue and makes itself cozy—hoping never to be found, which is unlikely since it will inevitably cause discomfort. These same traumas also get lodged in the body in other ways. For example, the *energy* of the **trauma stores in the *energy field,*** while *emotions* **related to such trauma store in the** *emotional body.* In any case, something painful and foreign to the body and soul gets locked in. Sometimes these hurts begin to fester. Other times, they tend to go numb. Still other times the pain remains completely present and tender to the touch. Finally, at other times, the pain remains present but places muscular armor around itself. In such circumstances, the armor can be lovingly touched and gradually broken down. Of course, this means that eventually there can be a sudden awakening of pain in the tissue. When this occurs during a sexual healing massage, begin holding the mental intention of love and healing as you back off slightly and rub gently. Then vibrate your finger or hold it completely still until it feels appropriate to move in again for more healing massage, which sometimes has to wait for another day.

Many individuals have sexual inhibitions or dysfunctions that include difficulty reaching an orgasm through intercourse alone. Sacred sexuality can be useful for healing such issues. **Although sexual healing may not be the primary focus of the sexual experience, sexual issues of repression or trauma can be brought to the lovemaking session and patiently addressed.** All such repressed or stored trauma can have an effect on a person's health and sexuality.

In most cases, the more often a woman has intercourse without taking the time to go through her natural stages of arousal and preparation, the thicker the tissue within her yoni becomes, thus decreasing her sensitivity. Furthermore, when she moves her pelvis too much, she unconsciously tightens her pelvic and vaginal muscles, which, once again, creates an unhealthy patterning in her sexual anatomy. Ironically, a woman may think she is sexually healthy and responsive to stimulation, but sometimes her arousal does not result from sexual health and vitality. Rather, it results from her sexual anatomy becoming hardened and giving off false signs of arousal. The male lingam can also become traumatized from physical and sexual abuse, as well as from excessive masturbation. For example, if a man gets used to quick ejaculations from fast-paced masturbation, he can become premature in his ejaculations. Excessive masturbation might also make his lingam numb to pleasuring by a partner.

Orgasms
Physical Orgasms

*T*he most common type of orgasm is the physical peak, orgasm, which usually results from direct stimulation of the penis or clitoris (the female's version of a penis). The physical orgasm results in an ejaculation of fluids and strong sensations within the muscles and nervous system, as well as a brief burst of energy in the pelvis. During this level of orgasm, there are similarities and differences between the physiological responses of a man and woman.

The most general similarity is that for both men and women, a physical orgasm is basically just an ejaculation. This means that both men and women experience an engorgement of blood to the genital region and a contracting of their muscles and internal organs, not dissimilar to preparing to sneeze, which is why a physical orgasm is sometimes referred to as a "pelvic sneeze." The man's testicles contract, as do the woman's clitoris and vaginal canal. The orgasmic buildup culminates as several quick, spasm-like contractions, followed by a release of energy and fluids. This "climax" of energy buildup and explosion is the most common form of orgasm.

There are two general stages (build-up and release) of a physical orgasm. These are activated by two different parts of the nervous system. The "arousal and stimulation" are connected to the parasympathetic portion of the autonomic nervous system. The "muscular contractions and orgasmic release" are connected to the sympathetic portion of the autonomic nervous system.

In addition to the physiological responses, there are deeper and more varied dimensions to physical stimulation and orgasm than most people are aware of. Although the clitoris and penis are the most commonly used keys to orgasm, orgasms can also be reached through the stimulation of other portions of the genitals, such as a woman's G-spot and a man's prostate. The same holds true for the various parts of the woman's yoni. A woman can have an orgasm by stimulation of her cervix, which is often triggered by insertion of the penis deeply enough to rub against the cervix. In fact, any part of the human body can reach an orgasm—as long as the recipient is receptive and there is proper stimulation.

Even though men and women have orgasmic similarities, there are differences as well. One such difference is the length of time it takes to build up to an orgasm and the duration of the orgasm. Another difference between the male and female orgasm is the short-lived, intense peak of the male orgasm. Women, on the other hand, have several levels and types of physical orgasms.

Some learned men . . . say that women . . . should not study the Kama Sutra. But . . . this objection does not hold, for women already know the principles of Kama Sutra.

—*Kama Sutra*

Energetic Orgasms

There is a point in your evolutionary development where orgasms move beyond physical, physiological experiences and into the next level—orgasms of your energy systems. Energy-system orgasms still involve the anatomy and all other aspects of physical orgasms, but more is added. Now you can take conscious control of physical stimulation and excitation and channel it throughout your body. Now you can control the sexual energy that ordinarily moves down and out of the body and redirect it inward and upward for rejuvenation and more advanced forms of orgasm. With energetic orgasms, it is possible to separate the sensations of an orgasm from the physiological ejaculation, thus allowing you to feel all the pleasures of having an orgasm without losing fluids or stamina.

Emotional Orgasms

As we heal from sexual traumas and inhibitions, our bodies and souls begin to feel liberated and therefore exhibit signs of letting go. This releasing can manifest in various types of orgasms—including emotional orgasms.

The best way to define emotional orgasms is to start by dividing them into two types. First, there can be moments of spontaneous emotional release expressed as panic or tears during the lovemaking experience. This type of emotional orgasm can also result in laughter, which is another way to release physical, energetic, and emotional tensions. Such symptoms indicate the surfacing of old, buried emotional traumas—even without conscious visions or memories. The releasing of these intense emotions is a form of orgasm—an emotional orgasm.

Despite their unpredictable onset and awkward timing (as well as any helplessness felt by either partner), these releases are very healing. After every emotional release, time should be taken for deep, calming breaths, while the person having the release focuses on, or connects with, the Spiritual Presence of Divine Love and safety.

The second type of emotional orgasm can be triggered by the relief and gratitude partners feel when realizing on some level that they are safe and healing. **This type of emotional orgasm can also be triggered solely by the deep, romantic connection felt by the partners who are sharing the experience of lovemaking.** These are tears of joy that result from the realization of the depths of love the partners feel for each other.

One way for lovers to experience an emotional orgasm is to create a deep level of connection through slow body movements and deep eye contact. When making love, gaze into each other's eyes as much as possible. If there is truly a loving intent between lovers, the two of them will notice a deepening of vulnerability and love. Eye-to-eye contact will dissolve the false masks that prevent true intimacy. So, lock eyes, kiss often, and verbally communicate by sharing your deepest feelings. There is a possibility that connecting this deeply with your current partner may feel uncomfortable. So don't force it! If you give it a try, you might discover that it proves healing to you both. But if you cannot do these practices, you might need to consider why you are making love to someone with whom you cannot communicate or even make eye contact.

Mental Orgasms

Mental orgasms can best be defined as orgasms that are reached either exclusively with images held in the mind *or* with the assistance of concentrated visualization. In the first example, the mind enhances physical stimulation, even to the point of an orgasmic release. In fact, many of the arts of sacred sexuality promote the use of the mind to evoke as much excitation as possible. Partners can increase each other's arousal through imagination by the use of erotically stimulating thoughts and words prior to, or instead of, actions.

The second possibility uses concentration and the skill of *projecting* your thoughts to another person for the purpose of sexual arousal. You do not have to be in physical contact with this person to succeed. The person you are thinking about can be on the other side of the room or the other side of the planet, for that matter. Distance is no obstacle! First, your mind can, and must, eliminate any thought or belief that distance is a barrier to oneness. Then, with enough focus, one lover can mentally arouse another—even to the point of orgasm. It helps for your partner to be simultaneously tuned in to receiving.

Soul-Level (Total-Being) Orgasms

Physiologically speaking, an orgasm is a build-up of sexual *fluids* waiting to be released upon climax. A soul-level orgasm, on the other hand, is a build-up of love-based *energy* waiting to be anchored, accepted, and released at the moment of surrendering to love's presence.

A soul-level orgasm occurs in one of two ways. The first way involves the building up of a physical, energetic, emotional, and spiritual connection until all sensation of the body disappears and the soul rises to the foreground. The second way to experience a soul-level orgasm is through the build-up of spiritual, energetic ecstasy to the extent that physical touch becomes unnecessary to achieve the orgasm. The latter way includes spiritual ecstatic experiences where a person rides waves of ecstasy that can take him or her into dimensions of the soul.

Energetic ecstasy and soul-level orgasms occur when a Spiritual frequency or vibration reaches down and stimulates, or caresses, a person's body (nervous system) and soul (heart-center), resulting in an ecstatic experience within the body. Although the body *can* be manually stimulated (without spiritual integrity or intent) to the point of creating an energetic (and *seemingly* ecstatic) response, this purely physiological experience cannot duplicate the feeling of complete oneness resulting from a soul-level orgasm.

Spiritual Orgasms

Of the few primary practices that lead to the experiencing of a spiritual orgasm, none can replace the daily practice and application of communing with God and living a life of loving service. A spiritual orgasm is a spiritual and physiological process that first takes place within the skull of your head and then fills your body.

Practicing advanced forms of meditation, breathwork, and in-jaculations are all valid ways to *assist* the process of a spiritual orgasm. Such exercises include the cobra breath (learned in Kriya or Tantric yoga), a technique never written down but only passed down through initiations between teacher and student. The cobra breath clears the etheric pathways within the *sushumna* (spinal) meridian. The vacuum created by this cleansing clears the way for energy and spinal fluid to rise from the sacrum and to the brain. The profound effects of true communion with God are not unknown to highly evolved mystics, Tibetan Buddhists, and advanced practitioners of meditation.

By regularly communing with God through meditation, you activate a tone, or vibrational frequency, at the center of your head. This (often imperceptible) tone awakens the kundalini energy (or *sushumna*) *and* cerebral spinal fluid at the base of the spine, beckoning it upward along the spine and then to the brain. At this point, cerebral spinal fluid fills the inside of the skull (cranium), creating an energy grid between the two hemispheres of the brain. This total-brain awakening also activates the sphenoid bone of the cranium, which, in turn, stimulates the hypothalamus and the pineal and pituitary glands. Then these glands send messages of love and healing, as well as orgasmic-light sensations, to other major glands and throughout your body.

Stimulation of the pituitary and pineal glands also creates an arc of light that illuminates your entire brain and skull (a part of the body that Taoists refer to as the "Original Cavity" or "Ancestral Hall"). This light-activation, results in the awakening of your mind's eye and your crown chakra, blasting energy up into the heavens. This "liquid-light" then pours over your forehead and down the front of your body, a process well described in the Bible's twenty-third Psalm which reads, "Thou hast anointed my head with oil; my cup runneth over. I will dwell in the house of the Lord forever."

The techniques and their effects for experiencing physical and energetic orgasms are merely preparations for attaining the supreme experience of spiritual orgasms. Ultimately, the practice and process of attaining spiritual orgasms are not dependent upon actual sexual contact. The primary purpose of practicing sacred sexuality has always been to achieve union, or a blissful dance with the Divine. Having now attained such union through spiritual orgasms, our consciousness is swept away into a sea of bliss unlike any that accompanies sexual orgasms. This bliss doesn't pass away with time but remains permanently encoded in our hearts and souls. Most of the exercises related to spiritual orgasms are done in the mind and *not* with the body. Nonetheless, the effects are felt, seen, and heard in body, mind, and soul.

Revelation . . . reflects the original form of communication between God and His creation, involving the extremely personal sense of creation sometimes sought in physical relationships. Physical closeness cannot achieve it.

—*A Course in Miracles*

The Afterglow
Postplay

*T*he afterglow is as much an essential part of the sacred sexual experience as any step leading up to this moment. The *postplay,* or afterglow, can be viewed as the opposite of *foreplay* because it involves "coming down," as opposed to "building up." Yet the afterglow has many of the same ingredients as foreplay *and* the actual sexual encounter—such as being present, communicating, connecting, and even physical contact. If properly treated, the afterglow can prolong the mood created during the precious moments of any sexual experience.

Sacred sexuality doesn't end with an orgasm or with the ecstatic experience of feeling waves of energy and universal love. Instead, the sacred sexual experience (like all sacred experiences) is meant to be integrated into your life and being—becoming a part of who and what you are. The time of postplay is a perfect opportunity to experience this integration.

During the afterglow, both partners are experiencing absorption of fluidic essences and a continuing exchange of energy. After the energy subsides, it's then time to share thoughts, feelings, and experiences. Later, the feeling of intimacy can be prolonged while washing up—perhaps with a sensual shower together. Even when it's time to get dressed, you can playfully assist each other, which continues the feeling of love, respect, and sacredness.

As communication helps to integrate all that was gained from the sexual experience into your relationship, grounding exercises help to integrate the energy from the sexual experience into the cells of your body. Therefore, getting grounded (and into your body) before attempting to interact with the outside world is the final stage of postplay and afterglow. All of the elements of foreplay (communicating, connecting, and grounding) make for an integrated experience that has permanent effects on your mind, body, and soul.

The repertoire for postplay involves more than just holding each other. Postplay also includes the following:

1. Coming Down
2. Remaining Present
3. Connecting
4. Expressing Appreciation
5. Cleaning Up
6. Communicating
7. Integrating

Coming Down

During the "coming down" phase of the sexual experience, lovers slowly regain their composure, and their breathing gradually returns to normal. Usually they experience a heightened state of relaxation and an inner state of calmness.

In some respects, the coming down phase is experienced alone, yet in other respects, it's experienced with your partner. Each partner needs to have "space" to release any leftover tension and absorb the continuing waves of energy. Then, gradually, as the lovers focus back into their present surroundings, they will be capable of being more present with each other.

Ecstasy is characterized by extreme peace,
tranquility, serenity, and radiant joy. [It is] a
blissful, tension-free state, a loss of ego boundaries
and an absolute sense of oneness with nature, with
the cosmic order, and with God.

—Stanislav Grof

Remaining Present

The concept of "being present" has been mentioned throughout this book as vital to any sacred sexual experience. But it's equally essential at the *closing* of a sexual encounter. By not rushing off into life's distraction—by remaining focused and present—now more than ever, you can demonstrate to your partner that he or she is a valuable being and a priority to you. This may be one of the most important messages you ever offer your partner.

Holding and Connecting

Generally, this vital moment of connecting is stereotypically considered to be more important to a woman than a man. Women are said to more often request being held after intercourse and miss it when it's not provided. If this is true, then the way a man deals with the afterglow period reveals much about his personal nature and psychological health. For example, if he falls asleep or rushes from the room, it might indicate a fear of deeper connecting, as well as unhealed phobias or negative beliefs about sex. Of course, just because he hangs around a little longer doesn't mean he's a saint—especially if he is doing so just to get more sex. But his ability to maintain a conscious presence after sex can reveal his commitment to a deeper, more authentic connection with his partner. For women, on the other hand, holding and connecting can be virtually the most important part of any sexual experience. In fact, **women**

often participate in sex simply to achieve a deeper level of connection and, sometimes, just for the holding.

Praise be to God who has placed the source of man's greatest pleasure in the woman's natural parts (genitals), and woman's greatest pleasure in the natural parts (genitals) of man.

—*The Perfumed Garden*

Expressing Appreciation

Now is your chance to assure your partner that all the effort he or she put into co-creating the sacred sexual experience was well worth it and appreciated. Do everything in your power to articulate and demonstrate how wonderful the experience was and how much you appreciate the sharing. Your appreciation can be conveyed through thoughts, words, and/or gestures.

Cleaning Up

Cleaning up after a sexual encounter is a delicate matter. You don't want to send your partner signals that imply you are ashamed of, or turned-off by, the remnants of lovemaking. However, it is wise for health reasons to cleanse the genitals as soon as possible after sex— particularly if oral sex is involved. This cleansing helps to reduce the chance of germ-related viruses and irritations. Since some women have an allergy to latex, she should be sure to wash off any residue if a condom was used.

Communicating

It's best not to rush into talking immediately after intimate encounters. Nevertheless, communication is helpful for both partners. Communication should always be loving, tactful, and accentuate the positives. It might be best to focus primarily on what worked well. To avoid the impression of complaining, wait until later to discuss what you wanted more of, or what could be improved. Absorb all feedback and allow it to enhance your knowledge and understanding of your partner (and yourself).

Integrating and Grounding

The integration process encompasses absorbing the love, energy, and essence of the experience shared with your partner. In some respects, integration is accomplished through the aforementioned stages of the postplay process—coming down, being present, connecting, gratitude, and communication. However, the integration process also includes cleaning up together, dressing each other, and doing grounding exercises. Becoming grounded helps you feel centered and present. It prevents the sleepiness some people experience after sex. It also prevents spaciness and integrates the aroused sexual energy into the bloodstream. The most basic form of grounding exercises involves slow yoga-like stretches—particularly of the legs.

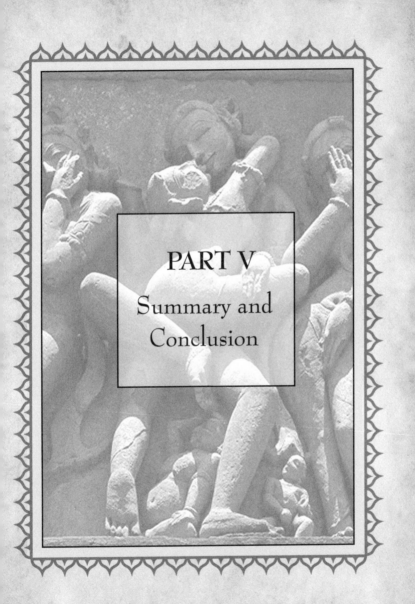

PART V
Summary and
Conclusion

Now for the Best Part

It Ends As It Began

*I*magine for a moment how your life (and sexual experiences) might have been different if you had been taught the concepts of sacred sexuality when you were a teenager. You will probably agree that your life would have been very different.

If you have read and absorbed any part of this book, you have already begun to integrate its information and goals. The more you integrate and practice the concepts taught, the more your life will change. You will have moments where you feel ecstatically alive and in harmony with your sexuality—a vital key to your health and well-being.

Reading the conclusion of this book may coincide with a new beginning for you. So allow the application and integration of this material to take you from knowledge in your mind to awareness in your soul. You will then emerge more spiritually connected and physically alive.

What is really so heartbreaking is that God has been with me all along, and I simply avoided His Presence. Yet now I can feel Him inside my heart, as closely as I feel my partner.

—Valerie Brooks *(Tantric Awakening)*

As you learn to balance and integrate the spiritual and physical aspects of your being, you will reach a level of empowerment of which most people only dream. You may find that others are attracted to you on various levels, so remember to maintain your center. Instead of responding to every attraction to or from others, empower *them* by being true to *yourself*. Demonstrate how to be loving, sensual, and passionate, yet responsible. Show others it *is* **possible to be fully alive in your body without compromising your soul.** Let others know that you see the wonderful qualities in them, as well as in yourself. You can choose to occasionally share your love and passion with others, but be clear that they must *earn* the right to touch your body (as you must earn the right to touch theirs). The body is the temple of the soul. It is sacred. *You* are sacred!

Throughout this book there have been reminders that, although the content speaks of sexuality, its goal is not sex, in and of itself. **Ultimately, this book uses sex as a metaphor for spiritual connection or at least as an arena for such a connection.** The intent is not to get you more caught up in your body, your senses, or shallow pleasures.

In truth, you *are not* and *do not* have a body. If you really did, your body would rule and limit you, but it does not, even though most of us believe to the contrary. Since you are not a body, sacred sexuality urges you to expand your awareness, connection, and understanding of who and what you are. Through use of the body, you are urged to discover a love and peace that surpasses the body's comprehension.

We are glorious, spiritual beings capable of experiencing bliss beyond the body's ability to contain. Therefore, all the words and concepts in this book, which seem to focus on the body and its sensations, are but the momentary honoring of the physical illusion. In other words, this book merely uses the body and sexuality as means for remembering the truth of the spirit. The sacred sexual experience becomes an arena in which to be playful, spontaneous, nonjudgmental, and above all, loving. This happens to be a perfect description for living a Divine embodiment. Sacred sexuality therefore returns us to the Garden of Eden, where we unite our hearts and souls with other people who are on the same journey Home. The sacred sexual experience is really about a remembrance that **we are the embodiment of the Love behind, and beyond, lovemaking.**

To the pure, all things are pure.

—Saint Paul (*Titus* 1:15)

PART VI

Appendix

An Outline of a Sacred Sexual Experience

The following chart provides a basic outline of a sacred sexual encounter. It can be photocopied and memorized or kept near at hand as a lovemaking guide.

I. SELF AWARENESS

1. Personal Centering and Self Observation–Loosen up the body and get centered.
2. Personal Hygiene–Cleanse your body thoroughly.
3. Self-Awareness–Acknowledge and prayerfully surrender any arising issues and inhibitions.
4. Visualization–Envision the kind of intimate encounter you would like to experience.

II. INTIMACY WITH OTHERS

1. Preparation–Prepare the environment. Include some candles, water, and perhaps fresh fruit.
2. Dedication–Take a moment to share some prayer or call in Divine Presence and acknowledge the divinity in yourself and your partner.
3. Cleansing–Take time to wash your body and sanitize your mouth.

4. Communication and Connecting–Discuss intent, boundaries, and preferences.
5. Massaging and Caressing–Practice variations of initial contact, massage, and genital stimulation.
6. Kissing and Mouthplay–Indulge in kissing, licking, and biting.
7. Oral Sex–Pleasure your partner as a buildup for intercourse *or* to the point of orgasm itself.

III. INTERCOURSE
1. Variations of Positions–Find the positions that work best for you and your lover.
2. Ejaculation Control–Practice the building up and holding off of orgasm.
3. Self-Awareness–Use various techniques to evoke orgasms.
4. Expand the Energy of the Orgasm–Whether you choose ejaculation or not, slow the orgasmic energy to spread it throughout your body.

IV. AFTERGLOW
1. Coming Down–Remain present and gracious.
2. Connecting–Take time to hold each other and connect.
3. Cleanup–Wash up or shower together.
4. Post-sex Communication–Discuss the experience and share feedback.
5. Grounding–Do stretches or take a walk to get grounded.

Terminology

The following is a clarification of terms used in this book. Some of the words listed are ancient Sanskrit, while others are Taoist. Each of these words includes a translation. In addition to the terms derived from ancient languages, this list also includes commonly used "crude" sexual slang along with the origins of such words. The purpose of including crude slang in a list of sacred terms is to enlighten the reader as to how seemingly irrational "street terms" often have rational origins.

Asanas–A Sanskrit term for yoga postures or sexual positions. Symbolic body mudras that place the practitioner in a receptive mode to receive Spirit.

Bandhas–(or locks) Specific muscle contraction exercises designed to seal off particular segments of the body, thus channeling energy into the desired segments of the body.

Blow Job–*Blo* is an old English term for prostitute. (slang for *fellatio*, or the oral pleasuring performed on a man's genitals).

Chakras–Sanskrit word for spinning wheel, or energy vortex, within the body that draws life-force from the ethers and into the body's organs and meridians.

Clitoris–(or jewel) A penis-like appendage that sits outside and above the opening of the vagina. It comes from the root word *clavis*, which means "key." The clitoris is clearly a key to a woman's experience of sexual pleasure and release.

Cock–Slang terminology for the erect, male penis, or lingam. It means "lifted and prepared to fire."

Cum (not "come")–From "a-cum-mulated" energy or substance. It refers to the energetic and fluidic release during orgasm.

Cunnilingus–The oral pleasuring performed on a woman's genitals.

Cunt–From *cunni*, which is a reference to the vagina. *Cunni* means "vagina."

Dakini–A Tantric guardian of the deeper mysteries. It usually refers to the female partner in the Tantric initiations or any human female who has achieved high levels of wisdom and awareness and is thereafter referred to as a goddess or *dakini*. The closest English version of the term would be "living angel" or "lightworker." All goddesses can be referred to as *dakini*, which means "sky walking woman." The male equivalent is referred to as a *daka*.

Deva–Sanskrit word for "god." *Devi* is a Sanskrit word for "goddess."

Ejaculation–Male ejaculations include the emission of semen, sperm, pre-cum, and other fluids upon orgasm. Female ejaculations are not experienced by all women; but when they occur, the ejaculate is made up of prostatic fluids from the paraurethral glands, fluids from the Bartholin glands, urine, fluids from the fallopian tubes, and other miscellaneous fluids.

Fellatio–The oral pleasuring performed on a man's genitals.

Fuck–Slang for intercourse. Believed to have originated from a law in the Middle Ages wherein a person was given legal permission to "fuck," or "Fornicate Under Consent of King."

G-spot–Originally called the "Grafenberg Spot"–also commonly referred to as the "G-oddess Spot." The G-spot is the female equivalent of the prostate and greatly contributes to vaginal (non-clitoral) orgasms, which occasionally include ejaculations in some women. Female ejaculations release fluids primarily from the paraurethral glands and ducts, located alongside of the female urethra, a region known as the urethral sponge.

In-jaculation–Turning an ejaculation inward.

Lingam–Sanskrit for "Wand of Light," referring to an erect penis. Another Tantric term for the penis is *vajra*, which means "thunderbolt." In Taoism–"Jade Stem" or "Jade Stalk."

Maithuna–A traditional, ritual practice of lovemaking.

Mantra–Sanskrit meaning "to focus the mind." A mantra is a sacred syllable or phrase that is repeated to focus the mind on the object of desire or worship.

Nadis–Term used in Tantra and yoga to indicate invisible "veins" that channel energy throughout the body to all organs and chakras. In Tantric tradition, it is believed that the body has 14 major *nadis* and 72,000 general *nadis*. The most important three (of the 14 major) *nadis*—running along the spine from tailbone to head—are *sushumna*, the central channel; *ida*, the left, feminine channel that ends in the left nostril; and *pingala*, the right, masculine channel that ends in the right nostril.

Namaste–A Hindu greeting that loosely translates as "I honor God within you and within me."

Om Mani Padme Hum–"*Om*" calls on the higher realms, *Mani* acknowledges the male principle, "*Padme*" acknowledges the female principle, and "*Hum*" refers to turning within oneself. It also translates as "Like a jewel in the center of the lotus, God is in the heart of me."

Orgasm–Means "to swell with excitement." It derives from the same root word as "orgy."

Panchamakara–Commonly known as the Tantric ritual of "the Five M's." This ritual involves several (usually at least eight) men and women practicing five traditional observances or rituals of partaking. In left-hand Tantra, they use *madya* (wine), *mamsa* (meat), *matsya* (fish), *mudra,* and *maithuna.* In some schools of right-hand Tantra, they substitute with coconut juice, cheese, ginger, rice, and honey.

Penis–A clinical term for the male organ/shaft.

Puja–Sanskrit for a sacred gathering or ceremony. In some styles of Tantra, a puja involves a group gathering, rituals, prayers, and worship but can also include sexual interaction.

Pussy–Cat fur–once used for masturbation (slang for "vagina").

Sanskrit–An ancient root language used throughout India and other parts of Asia and therefore the primary language used in ancient Hindu Tantra and modern Western Tantra.

Shakti–A goddess and Shiva's consort in the Tantric tradition. Also female sexual energy.

Terminology

Shiva–A god in the Tantric tradition. He is said to take on three forms–one of which is the lingam.

Tantra–Sanskrit for an art or tool for joining or weaving together.

Tantric Texts–Tantric scriptures are generally classified as either Hindu or Buddhist "Tantras." Although many of the original Tantras have been lost, there are several that still exist as translations. Besides the original Tantras, there are also several well-known classic texts that describe the practice of Tantra and sacred sexuality. Not nearly as old as the original Tantras, they include (1) the *Kama Sutra*, written by Vatsyayana, an ancient Indian text that served as a sex manual and has become the most famous of all Indian erotic works; (2) the *Ananga Ranga*, written by Kalyanamalla, which, similar to the *Kama Sutra*, deals with a variety of erotic and sexual subjects ranging from aphrodisiacs to sexual positions and the art of seduction; and (3) *The Perfumed Garden*, an Arabian work written by Sheikh Nefzaoui. *The Perfumed Garden* includes several erotic tales, as well as describing numerous sexual positions and techniques.

Yantra–A Sanskrit term for a sacred geometric symbol (similar to a mandala) infused with energy and used to enhance a practitioner's concentration, thus magnifying the effects of his or her tantric practices. A *yantra* is also used as a living alter, wherein a tantric practitioner calls forth the presence of a chosen deity to guide and assist with the ceremony at hand. The deity then resides within the *yantra* until released.

The most sacred of all *yantra* is the *sri yantra*, which depicts the interplay of masculine and feminine forces that dance the dance of creation throughout the universe. In the *sri yantra*, there is a small dot known as a *bindu* symbolizing the original spark that gives rise to the male and female polarity and to all of creation.

Yoni–Sanskrit for "Sacred Space"–the female sexual organs or vagina. In Taoism–"Jade Cavern" or "Jade Gate."

The *sri yantra*: the most sacred symbol in Tantra

Sexual Facts

This list is compiled from the latest research and surveys. While such facts are never a hundred percent accurate, the statements are nevertheless generally true. These details are certain to evoke varied responses and interpretations. It is possible to perceive a pattern of evolution regarding sexuality, demonstrated by the fact that in the last twenty years twice as many women report having orgasms. This is a quantum leap toward freedom from the sexual "dark ages." On the other hand, it might appear that we still have a need for greater sexual healing and education, which is demonstrated by the fact that ninety percent of teenagers in most high schools claim to have already had sex. Furthermore, most of the teenagers surveyed have reported that they failed to use condoms.

Aside from pointing out some dramatic facts about sex and sexuality, this information can also dispel misconceptions on the topic. It may prove comforting to know where you stand in relation to the statistics. It may also serve to motivate you to make some changes in your sexual experiences. If you find any of the noted facts to be doubtful, simply check the Internet or your local library resource center.

1. Over 90% of men and 70% of women masturbate.

2. Although women are capable of sexual pleasure, orgasm, and even ejaculation, this fact is still doubted by medical science.

3. Only 14% of women report having multiple orgasms.

4. As many as 37% of males have had at least one homosexual experience.

5. Only one out of ten women report a wonderful first sexual experience.

6. Only 30% of women report reaching orgasm during sexual intercourse, but over 80% reach orgasm during masturbation.

7. Sexually active adults worldwide have sex on an average of once every three days.

8. Nearly 50% of the world's adults have had a one-night stand.

9. Nearly 60% of women surveyed have faked an orgasm and just 15% of men.

10. As many as one in ten sexually active adults have had sex with their best friend's partner.

11. The average male reaches orgasm within five minutes.

12. The average male orgasm lasts only three seconds.

13. The average male penis is 3 inches (when not erect) and 5-6 inches (when erect).

14. The average depth of a woman's vagina is only about 4 inches, but it elongates during intercourse.

15. Well over half of all men and women surveyed report having experimented with such minor forms of bondage as wrist binding and blindfolding.

16. Well over half of all men and women surveyed report having experimented with some form of sex toy.

17. Less than 30% of sexually active adults report feeling comfortable talking dirty.

18. Although 75% of men have orgasms with their partners, only 30% of women can make the same claim.

19. By the age of fifty, nearly 40% of all males and 20% of females will have had an affair.

20. One in every three sexually active people will contract an STD by the age of thirty-five.

21. Recent reports claim that over 90% of high school students in the USA have had intercourse.

22. Nearly one in four women have been forced to perform a sexual act and nearly 95% of them claim to have known the perpetrator.

EXPLORING
SACRED SEXUALITY

Facilitated by Michael Mirdad, this workshop is a five-day intensive that synthesizes the most effective arts of sacred sexuality, including Tantra and Taoist sexology. This workshop also incorporates modern techniques of sexual healing. The event is for everyone, whether you are single, have a partner, are sexually active or not. In the safest and most sacred atmosphere, you will learn to develop and channel your own sexual energy to enhance health, vitality, and self-awareness.

THE WORKSHOP ALSO FEATURES:

- Exercises for health, vitality, and rejuvenation
- Techniques for enhancing the intimacy in your relationships
- Self-awareness to heal sexual guilt, shame, and inhibitions
- An introduction to sexual anatomy and terminology
- Tantric and Taoist techniques to enhance your sexual experience
- Techniques for channeling your sexual energy into creative ecstasy

To apply for this workshop, please contact us at
Grail Productions, PO Box 1908, Sedona, AZ 86339
For details: 360-671-8349 or office@grailproductions.com.

Visit us at www.SpiritualTantra.net

WORKSHOP INTENSIVES
Offered by Michael Mirdad

There are three primary workshop intensives offered by Michael Mirdad. The first, in the spring, is *Healing: Body and Soul* and is designed to bring the attendees to new levels of physical, emotional, and spiritual health, while also teaching them how to become healers (or better healers). The second, in the summer, is *Living Mastery*. This workshop is great for anyone who is ready to discover new levels of direction, responsibility, balance, and wholeness. The third workshop, in the fall, *Initiations Into Christ Consciousness*, teaches attendees to connect with their True (Christ) Self and deeper levels of spiritual awareness.

HEALING: BODY & SOUL

This workshop is a 5-day intensive for anyone seeking to receive physical and/or emotional healing or choosing to develop greater healing abilities. It is perfect for those wanting to renew their commitment to maintaining physical/emotional health and spiritual connectedness and includes training in herbology, massage, energy work, Tai Chi, acupressure, Reiki, emotional healing, yoga, cranial release, health intuitiveness.

"I am so grateful that the workshop re-ignited or deepened the healer in me. I absolutely loved using a combination of breath work, physical body work, intuition, and advanced techniques to trigger issues on a cellular level to bring them forth to be healed. We learned healing and counseling skills that most counselors don't even know!" –Ron, ONT

www.GrailProductions.com

LIVING MASTERY INTENSIVE

This workshop is a five-day intensive for those who are prepared to live a life of fulfillment. It teaches how to experience the best life possible in every aspect of living. No other single event offers so much! Living Mastery is an advanced training for students and teachers of spirituality who are ready to learn how to manifest a spiritual, integrated, balanced, and prosperous life, as well as learning how to bring God and all spiritual learning into their daily lives and activities. Topics include the following: physical mastery–manifesting prosperity, living healthy through yoga and diet, and training in several healing arts; emotional mastery–developing psychic abilities, creating fulfilling relationships, and learning advanced emotional healing techniques; mental mastery–developing greater focus, learning effective meditation, and discovering your soul's purpose; and spiritual mastery–developing a life plan, learning true forgiveness, awakening higher levels of consciousness, and opening your heart center.

"I am so honored to have had the opportunity to experience five of the most amazing days of my life, while attending the Mastery Workshop. I became aware of my strength and endurance through rock climbing, yoga, and the obstacle course. I embraced exercises in past life regression and emotional healing. I was challenged doing exercises in cloud busting and learning the importance of focusing, as well as dividing and conquering life's obstacles. And I learned the importance of prayer and meditation and letting God live through me every instant of my life." –Janet, NY

www.GrailProductions.com

INITIATIONS INTO
CHRIST CONSCIOUSNESS

This workshop is an advanced training for students and teachers of Christ Consciousness. It covers advanced teachings and spiritual concepts, as well as profound levels of application. Attendees learn to clear their centers of consciousness and live a life that reflects their higher self in mind, body, and soul. This workshop also covers the following: initiations into Christ Consciousness through rarely understood mystery teachings of Jesus–some of which were transferred to Mary Magdalene, clearing of various energy centers (chakras), the secret teachings of Christ, Jesus' missing years amongst the Essenes, and the Mystery Temples, and experiencing your own spiritual baptism.

"There were so many wonderful activities at this workshop. The information about the history of the universe was clear, informative, and intriguing. The closing initiation into the Christ Consciousness was transformative. When I lay down in the middle of the circle, I felt the amplification of energy, all the light, in my body. As my heart chakra opened, I felt as if my entire chest were being pulled up to the ceiling, while my breath was deep and being pulled through my body to my feet. I felt like I was in the zone of Jesus, Mary, and of course fellow attendees. I feel as though I have attained a new spiritual level." –Jean, OR

www.GrailProductions.com

ORDER FORM

To order any of our books or request more information on any of these publications, please copy and mail in this order form. You can also call our office or visit our website (see below) for a complete list of books, CDs, and DVDs.

Name_____

Address_____

City, State, Zip_____

Phone_____

Fax_____

Email_____

Please include any special instructions when ordering.
Please make checks payable to Grail Productions.

_____

_____

An Introduction to Tantra and Sacred Sexuality
_____ copies at $15.00 each =   _____

Healing the Heart & Soul
_____ copies at $15.00 each =   _____

Sacred Sexuality, A Manual for Living Bliss
_____ copies at $25.00 each =   _____

Seven Initiations of the Spiritual Path
_____ copies at $15.00 each =   _____

You're Not Going Crazy. . .You're Just Waking Up!
_____ copies at $15.00 each =   _____

Add $2.00 for S&H per book   _____

Total   _____

Grail Productions, PO Box 1908, Sedona, AZ 86339
For information: (360) 671-8349 or office@grailproductions.com
Visit us at www.GrailProductions.com

About the Author

*M*ichael Mirdad is a world-renowned spiritual teacher, healer, and author with an extensive background in spirituality and healing. He is the author of the best-selling books *Healing the Heart & Soul, Sacred Sexuality: A Manual for Living Bliss*, and *You're Not Going Crazy . . . You're Just Waking Up!* Michael is regularly featured as a keynote speaker at some of the world's largest conferences, as well as being on radio, television, and various Internet programs. In addition to being a cover story in Evolve Magazine, Michael has been featured in such magazines as *Yoga Journal*, *Sedona Journal*, and *Whole Self Times*.

Michael has traveled throughout the world conducting thousands of classes, lectures, and workshops on spirituality, relationships, and healing. He is one of the few teachers in the Western world with over 30 years of tantric teaching and practice and is the creator of "Spiritual Tantra" and "Middle-Path Tantra."

Michael's powerful and insightful private sessions have transformed the lives of thousands of clients. His vast knowledge and wisdom combined with his personal warmth, humor, and integrity have earned him the title of "Teacher's Teacher" and "Healer's Healer" from students, teachers, and authors around the world.